Policing, Accountability and Young People

Jennifer Hamilton, Katy Radford and Neil Jarman

Institute for Conflict Research
April 2003

First Published 2003
By Institute for Conflict Research
Unit 14, North City Business Centre
2 Duncairn Gardens
Belfast BT15 2GG
Tel: 028 9074 2682
Fax: 028 9035 6654
Email: info@conflictresearch.org.uk
www.conflictresearch.org.uk

ISBN 0-9541898-2-5

Produced by:
three creative company 028 9048 3388

Acknowledgments

We would like to thank all the young people, youth leaders and the various organisations who contributed to this research, without their co-operation this research would have been impossible. Your time, willingness and openness were very much appreciated.

We also wish to thank the Police Ombudsman's Office for Northern Ireland and the Policing Board for Northern Ireland for funding this research. A special thanks to Malcolm Ostermeyer and Tim Trimble (Police Ombudsman's Office) and David Wilson and Arthur Rice (Policing Board) for their support and encouragement throughout the research and publication of this report.

Finally, a thank you to all the staff at ICR for their assistance and patience throughout this research.

Contents

	Page
Executive Summary	5
Section 1 Introduction	11
Section 2 Methodology	21
Section 3 Demographic Breakdown of Survey Respondents	33
Section 4 Police Service of Northern Ireland	37
Section 5 Police Ombudsman for Northern Ireland	65
Section 6 Policing Board and District Policing Partnerships	79
Section 7 Suggestions from the young people	85
Section 8 Recommendations	89
References	93
Appendices	97

List of Tables and Figures

Table 1   Age breakdown of complaints against the police
Table 2   Current positions of respondents
Table 3   Areas surveyed
Table 4   Locations and participants of the focus groups
Table 5   Age and gender split of participants
Table 6   DCUs surveyed
Table 7   Religious background
Table 8   Ethnic background
Table 9   Educational qualification
Table 10   Opinions about the PSNI
Table 11   Opinions about the PSNI by community background
Table 12   Activities PSNI should be concentrating on
Table 13   Nature of contact
Table 14   Other forms of contact
Table 15   Satisfaction with PSNI during contact
Table 16   Types of unacceptable behaviour
Table 17   Organisation where complaint was lodged
Table 18   The role of the Police Ombudsman
Table 19   Opinions about the Police Ombudsman
Table 20   Reasons for not complaining
Table 21   Reasons not happy with service from the PONI
Table 22   The role of the Policing Board
Table 23   The role of the District Policing Partnerships

Figure 1   Support for the police by community background
Figure 2   The Board's impartiality by community background
Figure 3   The Board's independence by community background
Figure 4   Making policing more effective and efficient by community background

Executive Summary

This research focuses on young people's attitudes and experiences of policing in Northern Ireland and especially on the process of making complaints against officers in the PSNI. The research adopted both qualitative and quantitative approaches and the analysis is based on discussions within 31 focus groups and the findings of a questionnaire completed by 1163 young people across Northern Ireland.

The main issues addressed are the attitudes and knowledge of young people towards:
1. The PSNI, their experiences of that service, of differences between the PSNI and the RUC; and the scale and nature of problems experienced in interacting with the PSNI;
2. The Office of the Police Ombudsman, its work and responsibilities; their experience of making complaints about the police and changes that should be made to the system of reporting or processing complaints; and
3. The Policing Board and District Policing Partnerships.

The following are a summary of the main findings from the research.

Policing - main findings

Contact
- 41% of respondents had some contact with the police in the past 12 months.
- More males (56%) than females (28%) reported contact.
- Those living in urban regions had more contact than those in rural regions.
- 35% of respondents were either very satisfied or satisfied with the PSNI during this contact.
- Being stopped and questioned and being asked to move on were the two most frequently occurring forms of contact.
- Young people regard these types of contact as forms of harassment.

Police Behaviour and young people's experiences
- Young people's experiences of the police were predominantly negative.
- More young people agreed than disagreed that the police were honest, professional, helpful, there to protect them and acceptable.

- 24% of respondents were very dissatisfied with the PSNI.
- The main form of unacceptable behaviour reported was disrespectfulness and/or impoliteness (58%).
- Forms of harassment included physical violence, a constant police presence and being watched, confiscation of goods and verbal abuse.
- Young people voiced annoyance that it was always assumed that they were 'up to no good'.

Complaining
- 5% of the respondents had made a complaint about the police in the past 12 months.

Changes
- Some Catholic participants felt that there had not been enough changes to the Police Service.
- Many Protestants felt that there had been too many changes.
- More Catholics (23%) than Protestants (12%) felt that policing had improved since the RUC was renamed as the PSNI.
- Many young people voiced concern about the political nature of policing.
- In spite of concerns many felt that a police service was still required.

Support
- 32% of respondents did not support the police.
- More Catholic than Protestants were unsupportive (38% compared to 27%).

Joining
- Only 17% of respondents would consider joining the PSNI.
- Less Catholics (11%) than Protestants (23%) expressed an interest in joining.
- Catholics who did indicate an interest in joining were frequently discouraged by family and/or friends.

Police Ombudsman - main findings

Awareness and knowledge
- 52% of respondents had heard of the Police Ombudsman.
- Older participants and those in a higher educational bracket were more aware.
- Nearly three quarters (72%) recognised the role of the Police Ombudsman as 'investigating complaints against the police'.
- 11% of the respondents knew how to contact the Office with only 2% having actually done so.
- Of this 2%, 38% were happy with the service.
- Of those who were not happy the 2 main reasons were a slow response (33%) and a feeling that the complaint was not taken seriously (33%)

Complaints
- Of respondents who had complained about the police, 26% had lodged their complaint with a police station and 16% with the Police Ombudsman's Office.
- 26% were happy with the service offered by the organisation they had approached.
- In theory many young people felt that if an individual felt they had been unfairly treated then this should be enough to merit a complaint. However, the reality was viewed very differently.
- Most of the young people felt that for a complaint to be taken seriously the incident had also to be serious such as physical assault.

Attitude
- Both communities generally viewed the Police Ombudsman's Office in a positive way.
- More within the Catholic community (57%) than the Protestant community (43%) felt that the Ombudsman was necessary.

Accessibility
- The Police Ombudsman's Office was not seen as being accessible to those living outside Belfast.
- There was little knowledge of how the Office could be approached, especially through Citizens' Advice Bureaux.

Outcome
- For many the preferred final outcome of any complaint would be to see the police officer, against who the complaint was made, be disciplined to ensure that no one else would suffer.
- Others stated that they wanted 'guarantees that action would be taken' and to be kept informed whilst the investigation was being carried out.

Policing Board – main findings

Awareness and knowledge of Policing Board
- General awareness of the Policing Board was much greater than knowledge of what it did, with 65% of respondents having heard of the Board. However, discussions within the focus groups were limited due to lack of knowledge.
- Some participants confused the Policing Board with other organisations such as the Parades Commission.
- Older participants and those within a higher educational bracket had more awareness and knowledge.

Opinions and views of the Policing Board
- 22% agreed that the Board was impartial.
- 23% agreed that the Board was independent.
- 20% agreed that the Board had made policing more effective.
- Catholics were more likely to disagree with the above statements.
- Concern was expressed about those with criminal records, custodial sentences or members of a political party being involved in the Board.

Awareness and knowledge of DPPs
- Overall respondents were not familiar with DPPs with only 24% having heard of them.
- Of those who had heard 18% did not know what their role was.

Opinions and views of DPPs
- Young people within some communities felt that the DPPs would have to have some clear benefit for them before they would be prepared to participate or engage in anyway.

Main Recommendations

Police Ombudsman for Northern Ireland

1. An advisory group of young people should be convened to advise on how the Police Ombudsman's Office might make their information and services more accessible to young people.

2. There should be a wider range of outlets throughout Northern Ireland for people to lodge complaints and a promotion of those that already exist. A Police Ombudsman logo that could be used to advertise where to lodge a complaint.

3. The Police Ombudsman's Office should consider having offices outside of Belfast.

4. A standardised complaint registration form should be available for all individuals, agencies and organisations (solicitors, CABs, politicians) that forward complaints against police officers. This will assist PONI in their data collection and analysis.

5. The Police Ombudsman should consider creating a team to deal specifically with complaints by young people.

Policing Board

6. The Policing Board should begin an outreach programme to engage with young people through schools and youth organisations.

7. The Board should initiate ongoing consultation with young people on policing issues, either through a consultative body of young people, or through programme of devolved consultations or through regular surveys of young people's attitudes.

8. The Board should raise the issues in this report with the Chief Constable and work together to ensure the PSNI develops a programme that encourages more effective engagement between the police and young people.

9. The Board should also discuss how the current training programmes within the PSNI deal with the policing of young people. The Policing Board should task the PSNI to consider how these issues raised in this report can be addressed within recruitment training and training delivered through DCUs.

1. Introduction

1.1 Policing and Accountability

Policing in Northern Ireland has been a controversial issue since the foundation of the local administration in 1921. Over recent years the policing structures, practices and methods of accountability have been subjected to considerable criticism, scrutiny and review (Brewer 1992; Hamilton, Moore and Trimble 1995; Ryder 2000, Weitzer 1995). The calls for a fundamental change increased during the period following the paramilitary ceasefires of 1994 with wide-ranging recommendations being made for reform in all areas of policing activity (CAJ 1997; Ellison and Smyth 2000; McGarry and O'Leary 1999; Wright and Bryett 2000). The British Government responded by initiating a major review of the police complaints system by Maurice Hayes in 1995. His report was published in 1997. Then, in 1998, a broad ranging review of all aspects of policing was undertaken by the Independent Commission on Policing as part of the Good Friday/Belfast Agreement. The commission, chaired by Chris Patten, reported in 1999.

The Hayes Report reviewed the current system of dealing with complaints and recommended a new structure involving the appointment of an independent Police Ombudsman to replace the Independent Commission for Police Complaints and to some extent the work of the RUC Complaints and Discipline Branch (see O'Rawe and Moore (2000) and Weitzer (1995) for a review of the work of the ICPC). The new Office would have complete control of the process of investigating complaints against the police. The recommendations in the Hayes Report received widespread support from both politicians and the police and were reinforced in the recommendations of the Patten Report. The Office of the Police Ombudsman for Northern Ireland was formally established in November 2000.

The Independent Commission on Policing included a wider review of the current system of police accountability and recommended the creation of a Policing Board to replace the existing Police Authority. Under their proposals the Policing Board would include a mix of political representatives and independent members, would be responsible for holding the police service publicly to account by providing an effective and democratically based oversight of policing and would work to create a close partnership between the police and local communities. The first meeting of the Policing Board took place in

November 2001. The Board has responsibility for producing a policing plan that determines operational, crime and justice strategies and has statutory responsibility 'to keep itself informed of trends and patterns' in complaints against the police (Policing Board Annual Report 2001-2002).

One of the central aims of the overall police reform process then has been to make the Police Service of Northern Ireland more accountable to all sections of the community for its strategy, its performance and the attitudes and behaviour of its officers. Thus it attempts to increase the legitimacy of the policing structures and police officers amongst those who are policed by the PSNI and those who the PSNI are responsible for serving and protecting. The Policing Board and the Office of the Police Ombudsman are the two bodies tasked with oversight of the key areas of police activity.

The September 2002 Northern Ireland Omnibus Survey indicated that only 8% of people thought that the standard of policing had improved in the past year, with 69% claiming it had remained the same. However, only 22% felt that the police did a poor or very poor job in their area, while 73% felt that the police treated Protestants and Catholics equally. The survey also revealed that young people were more critical of the police on these issues than older people. It also demonstrated that young people were less aware of some of the new structures such as the Policing Board and the District Police Partnerships than older generations but the results nevertheless indicated that 80% of young people had heard of the Policing Board and 77% thought the Board was working well.

Similar, recognition rates have also been recorded for the Police Ombudsman. The February 2002 Northern Ireland Omnibus Survey indicated that 86% of people had heard of the body and although this figure dropped to 66% among young people, awareness of the Ombudsman in the 16-24 age range was rising steadily. A high percentage of people also accepted that the Ombudsman was independent of the police and a majority in both communities felt the Office would help ensure the police did a good job.

The recent surveys suggest that there is both a high recognition of the new structures that have been introduced to hold the police to account, an acceptance that these structures are independent of the police and that they have been effective in their objectives. However it is significant that on all of these issues, young people are less positive than older people.

1.2 Police and Young People

The two primary areas where police legitimacy and accountability have been perceived as being most problematic are among the working class Catholic/nationalist communities and, to a lesser extent, among the working class Protestant/loyalist communities. However some acknowledgment has also been made of the often hostile and suspicious relationship that exists between the police and young people and in particular between the police and young working class males (Ellison 2001; McVeigh 1994). Although this tension and antipathy is in part consequential on the political context of Northern Ireland, it is also a mirror of the uneasy relationship between young people and the police in other similar industrial societies (Lee 1998; Loader 1996; Muncie 1999; Pinderhughes 1998).

The relationship between young people and the systems and structures of social order is often a difficult and problematic one. The adolescent years are the time when young people are most likely to be drawn into criminal activity (although this is often of a minor nature), or when they are most likely to engage in behaviour which challenges and confronts the established structures and agencies of authority, whether at familial, communal or societal level (Hartless et al 1995; Stol and Bervoets 2002). This means that young people are frequently both the subject and object of interest of the broader criminal justice system.

Although some young people may become involved in criminal activity, others are frequently regarded with suspicion simply because they are young or because they spend time hanging out on the streets with their friends. Some considerable degree of police activity is spent on 'keeping people in their place' as part of the process of maintaining state authority and imposing order (Waddington 1999). The increased interest by structures of authority in the behaviour of young people in turn helps to generate and reproduce antipathy, hostility and resentment by young people towards those in positions of authority, thus helping to sustain a reciprocal process.

In Northern Ireland young people are often regarded with fear, suspicion and mistrust (NIO Statistics and Research Branch 2003). They may be seen as both threatening and intimidating, as perpetrators of anti-social behaviour, of social disruption and as instigators of sectarian tensions and disorder (Jarman and O'Halloran 2001; Jarman et al 2002). Such feelings and suspicions may arise from little more than having groups of young people hanging around on street corners or marginal spaces. Their regular collective presence in public places readily attracts the attention of the police and 'community leaders' and this attention in turn encourages feelings of being harassed and picked upon, and may lead to a further sense of alienation from state and adult authority.

The Chief Constable's Annual Report reveals that the number of juvenile referrals (involving young people aged 17 and under) increased by just over 17% between 1998-99 and 2000-01 - from a figure of 10,988 in 1998-99 to 12,862 in 2000-01. These figures thus indicate a substantial and growing level of engagement between the police and young men and women. However the figures also reveal that in the year 2000-01, 20% of these cases led to no further action, 50% were concluded with advice or a warning and only 443 cases, or 3% of the total, resulted in a prosecution.

On one hand these figures may reflect a sensitive style of policing which aims to keep as many young people as possible out of the formal criminal justice system (evidenced by police interest in models of restorative justice). On the other hand it may lead to feelings among some young people that they are being picked upon for no good reason in a similar way to the use of the 'Sus laws' against young black males in England in the 1970s and 1980s (Scarman 1981, Cashmore and McLaughlin 1991).

Research on this broad issue indicates that many young people do in fact have an uneasy relationship with the police in Northern Ireland. McVeigh (1994) revealed that over one quarter of all young people had experience of some form of 'harassment' by the security forces, although working class Catholics were most likely to complain of this type of behaviour. More recently Ellison (2001) indicated ongoing concerns and resentment among many young people towards the police, which in part at least is caused by a sense of being harassed and confronted by police officers on a routine basis.

Recent PONI surveys support these findings. A survey of people's knowledge of complaints procedures and experiences of the police in October-November 2000 revealed that 20% of 16-24 year olds stated that the police had behaved in an unacceptable manner towards them, while a second survey in February-March 2001 indicated that 24% had experienced unacceptable behaviour by the police (Police Ombudsman's Office 2001a, 2001b). This second survey also showed that young people were more likely to experience such treatment at the hands of the police than older age cohorts. 17% of the total sample stated they had experienced unacceptable behaviour in dealing with the police compared with the 24% of 16-24 year olds. Furthermore, the survey revealed experience of a wide variety of unacceptable behaviour ranging from a lack of politeness to harassment and even violence. However, the methodology of quantitative surveys does not permit more detailed investigation of such experiences.

A high proportion of respondents to the survey were aware of the procedures for making a complaint against the police and of the existence of the Police Ombudsman's Office as an independent body. But only 4% stated that they would take a complaint against the police to that Office, compared with 44% who said they would complain directly to the police. Furthermore only 17% of those people who had actually experienced 'unacceptable behaviour' from the police did actually make a formal complaint. This data therefore suggests that while a wide range of people, and in particular young people, continue to have bad experiences in their encounters with the police, only a small percentage of these choose to publicise these experiences and make any form of formal complaint.

Information from the Police Ombudsman's Office also indicates that a high proportion of those young people who did make an initial complaint did not choose to follow this up or respond to requests for further information. Such data and information suggests that there is both a continuing problem in the relationship between the police and young people and also unwillingness among young people who experience unacceptable behaviour at the hands of the police to pursue a formal complaint against the PSNI.

1.3 Making Complaints

In recent years the issue of how best to deal with complaints against the police has come under increasing scrutiny from academics, policy makers and those involved in the criminal justice system (Goldsmith and Lewis 2000; Lewis 1999; McLaughlin and Johansen 2002). These studies have addressed a wide range of differing aspects of the complaints ethos, rationale and process across a number of countries. Some considerable debate has taken place on the most appropriate form for dealing with complaints, and whether these should be addressed internally by the police themselves or by an independent civil office. This was a fundamental issue for the Hayes Review, which acknowledged the need for any system both to be independent and to be seen to be independent, to have complete control of the complaints process, to be appropriately resourced, to be fair and accepted as fair to both complainant and police officers and to be open, accountable and transparent in its work (Hayes 1997). The Patten Report acknowledged that the Police Ombudsman system recommended for Northern Ireland would be among the more innovative and transparent approaches, that Hayes' model had been drawn on for the South African Police Complaints Commissioner and was in line with standards of best practice that either have been established elsewhere (Patten 1999:36-38) or were being proposed as part of a reform of the current system (Donnelly and Scott 2002).

While the appropriate form and structure of the complaints system has been a key area of debate, many other aspects of the system have also been critically examined. Several reviews have focused on issues arising from the workings of the complaints system, these include analysis of the nature and type of complaints received (Cotton and Povey 1999, 2000; Russell 1976), the views of complainants on police behaviour and the responses to complaints that have been made (Brown 1987; Smith 2001; Walker 1999; Waters and Brown 2000), the appropriateness of informal approaches to dispute resolution (CAJ 1997; McLaughlin and Johansen 2002) and the fairness and overall working of the complaints system in England and Wales, Scotland, Norway and in the USA (Maguire and Corbett 1991; HMIC for Scotland 2000; Thomassen 2002; Palmiotto 2001). A key outcome of this work has been to draw out some general details of the type of person who makes a complaint, what they complain about and levels of satisfaction with the process for addressing the complaint.

Research into the details of who makes complaints against the police, from Canada, Norway and the USA, has identified the stereotypical complainant as a single, unemployed male, under the age of 30 and who has at least one prior arrest (Thomassen 2002:205). Data from England and Wales similarly identify young males as prominent complainants. For example the Police Complaints Authority Annual Report for 2001-2002 notes that 27% of the 2678 complaints they recorded came from people under 25, while a study of complaints from police forces across England and Wales recorded that 49% of complainants were under 30 (Maguire and Corbett 1991). The research also clearly identified the issue of illegal use of physical force as the single largest category of complaints against police officers, particularly among the younger age groups – in Norway for example 21% of complaints cited use of force (Thomassen (2002:204). Finally, the overall view is that a substantial proportion of complainants were dissatisfied with key aspects of the process, and in particular the length of time taken to resolve a complaint, the degree to which complainants are kept informed of developments and the perceived independence of the investigation (Waters and Brown 2000).

The evidence from Northern Ireland is in line with many of these general trends. Figures for complaints made to the ICPC for 1993-1995 reveal that in approximately 45% of cases the complainant cited the use of force as an issue (Hayes 1997:104), while under the Police Ombudsman system around 49% of complaints mentioned one of a variety of forms of oppressive behaviour, with 38% complaining of assault (Police Ombudsman Annual Report 2000-2002:25). Hayes also noted all of the complaints cited above (duration, information and independence) related to the process of investigation as issues creating dissatisfaction and distrust in the ICPC system. The Police Ombudsman's Office has made prominent attempts to respond to such concerns and has set transparent targets in relation to responding to complaints, contacting complainants and completing investigations (Annual Report 2000-2002:49-53). Furthermore recent surveys carried out for the Police Ombudsman have indicated a growing awareness of the Office and acknowledgement of its independence from the formal policing structures (Police Ombudsman's Office 2001a, 2001b, 2002).

Statistics on the age and status of complainants also indicate similar patterns to those found elsewhere. Data from the Police Ombudsman's Office reveals that in 34% of cases where the age is known the complainant was under 24, with 19% of these being between 16 and 20 year olds. They indicate that 82% of 16-20 year olds and 70% of 16-24 year olds complained of some form of 'oppressive behaviour' (the broad category that includes assault and harassment). This compares with 41% of those 25 and over who cited oppressive behaviour as the issue at hand.

Table 1 Age Breakdown of Complaints Against the Police

	Percentage		
	16-24	25 +	Total
Oppressive Behaviour	70	41	51
Incivility	12	18	16
Failure of Duty	9	26	20
Other	9	15	13

The statistics also reveal that 86% of 16-24 year old complainants were male (as opposed to an average of 71% of those 25 and over) and indicate that 94% of people under 30 who made complaints were single and 74% of them were unemployed (compared with 23% of all complainants). The Police Ombudsman's Office statistics do not have data for prior arrests. The Northern Irish figures therefore also indicate that the most frequent complainant is a single, unemployed male between the ages of 16 and 30, with those under 24 being the largest proportion.

The statistics from the Police Ombudsman's Office reveal that young people are also more likely to make a complaint about behaviour that occurred in the street than older people (37% - 25%), while older people are more likely to complain about behaviour in a police station or in a domestic residence. Complaints by young people are also more likely to refer to events that occurred between 9 pm and 6 am (52% of all complaints) and at weekends (44% on a Saturday and Sunday) than those over 24.

The statistics show that young Catholics and Protestants have logged a similar percentage of complaints in their age range, although in the vast majority of cases (67%), the community background has not been recorded. Overall 26% of cases were made by Protestants and 20% by Catholics while in 48% of cases the community background is unknown.

It is perhaps not surprising that the largest number of complaints against the police in Northern Ireland come from young men, and that similar patterns are found in other western industrial societies, however, it is surprising that little attention has been paid to this fact by those carrying out research or analysis in this area. Some degree of recognition has been paid to issues of the class background of complainants (Russell 1976) and to ethnic identity or race factors in police community relations (Bowling and Phillips 2002; McLaughlin 1991) but little interest has been shown in the preponderance of complaints against the police from young people. This research report is breaking new ground in its focus upon the issue of young people and the reformed policing structures in Northern Ireland.

The report looks in some detail at the broad issue of attitudes of young people towards the police, their experience of the PSNI and how attitudes and experiences have changed over recent years. It also looks at young people's awareness, knowledge and experience of the structures of accountability that have been put in place since 2000. The primary area of focus is the experience that young people have of the Office of the Police Ombudsman, what they know of the process of making complaints, what experience they have of this process and whether they think this could be improved and if so what ideas they might have for making improvements. It also addresses many of the issues raised in the Hayes Report in relation to how complaints are dealt with, how well people are kept informed about how their complaint is being dealt with and how far the Police Ombudsman is seen to be independent. In addition the report looks at the awareness young people have of the Policing Board and how far that body is seen to be fulfilling its responsibilities.

The research, which is based upon both focus group discussions and analysis of a self-completion questionnaire, aims to provide data drawn from a much broader range of young people than most other recent surveys and adds substance and depth to the statistical data that has been available to date.

2. Methodology

2.1 Introduction

This research focused on young people's attitudes and experiences of policing in Northern Ireland and especially on the process of making complaints against officers in the PSNI. The research was initiated by the Police Ombudsman's Office to look at all aspects of young people's attitudes to and knowledge of the complaints process. The Policing Board were interested in a wider range of general attitudes to policing. The methods adopted included both qualitative (focus groups and interviews) and quantitative (questionnaires) enabling a larger sample of opinions to be obtained.

Three main issues have been addressed throughout the research:
1. The attitudes of young people to the PSNI, their experiences of that service, any differences that have been noted between the PSNI and the RUC and the scale and nature of problems that they have experienced in interacting with the PSNI;
2. The attitudes of young people to the Office of the Police Ombudsman for Northern Ireland: their knowledge of that Office, its work and responsibilities, their experience of making complaints about the police and any changes that they feel could be made to the system of reporting or processing complaints; and
3. The attitudes and knowledge of young people to the Policing Board and District Policing Partnerships (DPPs).

2.2 Age Range

The participants selected for investigation were between 16 and 24 years of age although some participants were below the age of 16 (10%). This age range was chosen as both the Police Ombudsman's Office and the Policing Board have found the opinions of this age group difficult to obtain. In addition the Police Ombudsman receive 34% of their complaints from 16-24 year olds. Therefore, it was felt that the experiences, opinions and views from this cohort were very important.

The researchers had difficulty accessing 16-24 year olds who were not in full time education. Other research studies have only focussed on those in full time education (Ellison 2001) and many have acknowledged the difficulty of including young people outside of educational establishments. To help overcome the problem the researchers in this study specifically targeted various groups with members who were either unemployed or in full time employment. Groups that we targeted included: youth training schemes, The Princes Trust, Hydebank Young Offenders Centre and various youth clubs and organisations throughout Northern Ireland. In spite of these efforts the sample still has a high proportion of young people from within educational establishments (Table 2).

Table 2 Current positions of respondents

Current Position	Frequency	Percentage
University	407	35
College	286	25
School	192	17
Full time training	120	10
Employed	80	7
Unemployed	45	4
Other	30	2
Total	1160	100
Missing	3	0.3

2.3 Methods

The research involved:
- a broad range of focus groups and self completion questionnaires covering the experiences of all major communities;
- both urban and more-rural locations;
- the experiences of both males and females; and
- the views of members of minority ethnic communities and socially excluded young people.

The self-completion questionnaires were delivered to a broad and representative range of educational establishments, including secondary schools, Further and Higher Education Colleges, training centres and the universities. Youth Councils, community youth groups, training schemes and the young offenders' centre were also targeted.

Questionnaire

The self-reported questionnaire is considered one of the most widely used research techniques due to the fact it can obtain a large sample in a relatively short period of time. When using the questionnaire as a research tool, care has to be taken, especially in selection of question types, question writing, the design, piloting, distribution and the return of the completed questionnaires (Bell 1993). A pilot test was conducted to ensure that any specific problems within each of these areas could be eradicated.

Design

The questionnaire was designed in conjunction with both the Police Ombudsman's Office and the Policing Board. Questions previously used in surveys already administered by the Police Ombudsman (Public Awareness of the Northern Ireland Police Complaints System 2000, 2001, 2002) were incorporated and/or amended as necessary. Considering the age group being surveyed it was felt that the questionnaire had to be a maximum of four pages and carefully worded so that its contents would be accessible to participants from all educational levels. All the members of the advisory group (representatives from the Police Ombudsman's Office, Policing Board and ICR) viewed the questions and an agreed questionnaire was obtained (Appendix 1).

The Pilot

A pilot test was carried out on 62 young people mainly between 16 and 19 from an integrated school with a range of educational abilities. The findings from the pilot are included in the final report. The pilot indicated that amendments were not necessary although various words (e.g. 'impartial') had to be explained to some participants. However, it was felt that these terms could not be removed from the questionnaire on this basis. For groups recognised as having lower literacy skills the questionnaire was read and assistance available. The questionnaire took between 10 and 20 minutes to complete.

The Sample

The questionnaire was completed by all focus group participants and then also distributed to a broader range of young people to get a wider spread of views. To obtain the sample (N=1163) for the survey, locations within the five Educational and Library Boards in Northern Ireland were targeted with at least two locations within each of these areas chosen. More groups were targeted within Belfast to give a spread of data between North, South, East and West Belfast.

Every effort was made to ensure the data was spread in terms of location, age, gender, community background and educational attainment. The sample was monitored throughout the data collection and when gaps were noted various groups were targeted to rectify the imbalance. Various cohorts were also specifically targeted namely members of the gay and lesbian, Traveller and Chinese communities, and young offenders. However, some of these groups were reluctant to participate due to feeling that they had been over researched in recent years. Representative groups from the lesbian, gay and bisexual community and the Traveller community chose not participate for this reason although some Travellers participated in some of the other groups. Table 3 shows the areas that were surveyed although catchment areas extended beyond these regions.

Table 3 Areas surveyed

Educational and Library Board	Area
Belfast	North
	South
	East
	West
North Eastern	Ballymena
	Coleraine
	Glengormley
	Larne
	Portrush
South Eastern	Downpatrick
	Bangor
Southern	Craigavon
	Dungannon
	Newry
	Portadown
Western	Derry/Londonderry
	Enniskillen
	Omagh

The Procedure

Organisations and groups were contacted initially by phone and then by follow up letter and/or personal visit requesting their participation in the questionnaire (and if possible focus group). On receiving agreement researchers visited the establishment /organisation and conducted a questionnaire, remaining with the participants while they completed it. Within some organisations supervised support was also given to the respondents. Before completion the research was explained and any questions/queries answered. Some establishments, such as some departments within the universities and one community group requested the questionnaire be left and completed by the young people in their own time to reduce disruption to their own activities. Although this was not ideal the researchers fully briefed the individuals distributing the questionnaire and were in close contact should any problems occur. Participants also had information on the questionnaire to refer to. The groups who opted for this fully co-operated in returning completed questionnaires and provided feedback on the process.

For participants under 18 a consent form was available for the organisations to send out prior to the researchers administering the questionnaire. Completion of the questionnaire was not compulsory and anyone who wished not to take part was given the option. All candidates were made aware of the potential value of the research and its anonymous and confidential nature.

Coding and Analysis

Each questionnaire was coded with a code relating to the organisation/school /university, and which was known to only the researchers. The questionnaire responses were coded and manually inputted into SPSS by a Belfast based research consultancy firm. A complete SPSS data sheet was produced and analysis, including frequencies and crosstabulations, conducted on SPSS.

Limitations of the questionnaire

Although it was felt that the questionnaire fully covered the main areas under investigation, there were limitations in that it required participants to self-report, which was problematic for those with lower reading and writing skills. However, the researchers did offer assistance to any individuals who had difficulty completing the questionnaire. The questionnaire did not provide the opportunity to explore various issues further as no substantial open questions were included, although the combination of qualitative and quantitative methods enabled further exploration of issues within the focus groups.

When designing the questionnaire a discussion took place concerning the inclusion of a 'don't know' category within some questions. It was decided not to include this option and the 'neither agree nor disagree' option was available. However, some young people found this confusing and if the questionnaire were to be repeated the researchers would now include the 'don't know' category to reduce confusion.

Focus Groups

The focus groups enabled opinions, attitudes and knowledge to be further explored. To guide the discussions themes and exploratory questions were developed within the advisory group.

Participants

The members of the focus groups were obtained through various schools, universities, colleges, training programmes and youth groups (including youth clubs and organisations that had contact with young offenders or youths perceived to be at risk of offending[1]) throughout Northern Ireland. Again the Education and Library Boards were used to ensure a spread of locations. As with the questionnaire it was intended that all ages, genders, community backgrounds and educational levels should be represented. Payment was offered to formally constituted groups to cover costs such as heating and transport, this was only taken up by a small number of groups.

In total 18 locations were targeted with 31 groups completed and a total of 242 participants. The groups were mainly composed of young people of mixed gender and background although some groups were single identity. Table 4 shows the areas targeted and the breakdown of the groups in terms of age and gender.

---

[1] Throughout this report, those young people acknowledged as being offenders or at risk of offending were members of focus groups where their potential participation had been initially identified by representatives from PBNI, NIACRO or HM Prison Service. The choice of whether or not to contribute to the research was made by individual participants

The Procedure

Whenever possible the groups were co-facilitated however, on occasions this was not convenient due to more than one group being conducted at that time. The research was explained to the group with any questions or queries answered. Before the discussions commenced the participants were requested to complete the questionnaire. The discussions were taped when possible but on occasions this was not ideal either because of background noise or the group not welcoming their discussions being recorded. When recording was not possible, detailed notes were made on a flipchart or by a co- facilitator. Themes and issues were raised within the group and discussions lasted between 45 and 90 minutes depending on each group. The facilitator's input was kept to a minimum throughout the discussions. Within some groups consent forms were provided to ensure that all participants fully understood the nature of their participation in the research.

Table 4 Locations and participants of focus groups

Education and Library Boards	Area	Total	Gender	Ages	Community Background
Belfast	Short Strand	10	7 male 3 female	Under 16x6 16x2 17x2	Catholic
Belfast	Lower Shankill (x2)	17	15 male 2 female	Under 16x8 16x3 17x3 20x3	Protestant
	Upper Shankill (x2)	17	12 male 5 female	16x10 17x6 20x1	Protestant
Belfast	Whitewell (x2)	21	10 male 11 female	16-18x21	Mixed
Belfast	Monkstown	5	5 male	16x1 17x2 18x2	Protestant
Belfast	(x2)	18	6 male 12 female	16x2 17x5 18x5 19x5 20x1	Mixed
North Eastern	Larne (x2)	18	8 male 10 female	Under16x10 16x2 17x3 18x2 19x1	Mixed
North Eastern	Ballymena	8	7 female 1 male	16-18x2 19-21x5 22-24x1	Mixed
North Eastern	Glengormley /Antrim	7	4 female 3 male	16-18x4 19-21x1 22-24x2	Mixed

Education and Library Boards	Area	Total	Gender	Ages	Community Background
Southern	Craigavon	8	5 male 3 female	16x1 17x2 18x2 19x2 24x1	Mixed
Southern	Dungannon	5	5 male	16x2 17x1 18x2	Catholic
Southern	Portadown	9	7 male 2 female	Under 16x7 16-18x1 19-21x1	Mixed
Southern	Newry	10	4 male 6 female	Under 16x4 16x4 17x2	Mixed
Western	Derry Londonderry	11	5 male 6 female	16-18x2 18-21x5 22-24x4	Mixed
	2 individual	5	2 male 3 female	16x1 17x1 19x2 24x1	Catholic
		10	9 male 1 female	16x1 17x5 18x3 19x1	Mixed
		4	4 male	20x2 22x1 25x1	Catholic
		3	3 female	22x1 23x1 24x1	Mixed
Western	Omagh	7	6 female 1 male	16-18x1 22-24x6	Mixed
Western	Enniskillen	15	7 female 8 male	16-18x6 19x1 16-18x8	Mixed

29

Methodology

Education and Library Boards	Area	Total	Gender	Ages	Community Background
1 individual				Mixed	
South Eastern	Downpatrick	9	3 male 6 female	17x2 18x3 19x4	Mixed
Chinese Community		6	3 female 3 male	16-18x6	Other
Hydebank Young Offenders	3 groups	5	5 male	18x4 20x1	Mixed
		6	6 male	17x3 19x1 20x2	
		8	8 male	15x1 18x1 19x1 20x5	

Limitations of the focus group discussions

Many of the groups participating were organised groups with youth leaders and on occasions these leaders were present throughout the discussions. It was felt that sometimes the discussions were hindered by the adult presence or steered in a particular way by the adult. These leaders were also the 'gate-keeper' between the researchers and the young people and at times the researchers were concerned that some individuals may have been forced or coerced into participating. However, it has to be emphasised that in general the young people willingly participated and eagerly contributed to the discussions. The focus group discussions give a snapshot of the experiences of some young people in Northern Ireland and in spite of these limitations were very worthwhile with few difficulties being noted.

2.4 Issues

Confidentiality

In conducting this research issues of confidentially were patently relevant to the researchers' use of the information and material disclosed. Some research participants' willingness to engage in the research was dependent upon the reassurance of discretion and confidentiality around various concerns. The concerns most frequently cited were that:

- those with extended family ties to the police would be compromised or endangered by taking part and;
- those who perceived themselves to be known to the policing organisations were concerned that information would feed back in some way and result in (further) police harassment.

These concerns are further problematised by the security situation in Northern Ireland. McVeigh (1994) recognises that issues of secrecy have perhaps been inevitable due to the very real physical threat not just to serving officers but also to their families and to those civilians with even the most tenuous connections to the security forces. Policy and practices of secrecy within policing organisations and those connected to them have undermined the confidence of communities already disenfranchised from the police (Hamilton et al 1995). Consequently, issues of confidentiality and secrecy that are perceived by some to be necessary to safety are seen by others to be dangerous, equated to a lack of openness, transparency and accountability. The culture of confidentially and concealment that is perceived by many to exist around matters pertaining to the security forces has increased feelings of mistrust and defensiveness between some individuals and those with connections to policing organisations through extended family ties.

Due to these concerns, on occasions the researchers had to reassure groups that they were independent of the police and associated bodies and that all information provided would be treated with confidentiality.

Sensitivity

In addition to confidentiality, the researchers were aware of the sensitivity of the subject matter and how various groups might perceive the research. This was of particular concern within groups with representatives from both Catholic and Protestant backgrounds. At times group members were willing to discuss issues openly but on occasions individuals were more reserved, mainly in groups where they did not know each other very well. On these occasions the researchers suggested to the group that if anyone wished to discuss any issues further individual interviews could be arranged. However, only a few individuals (N=3) were willing to be interviewed individually.

Participation

Some groups that were approached were not willing to participate in the research. This was either due to the nature of the discussions, which they perceived to be controversial for their group, or due to the source of the funding (Catholic Derry), or because they felt that they had been over-researched (Protestant East Belfast and Travellers). Some of those groups who felt that they had been over-researched recognised the importance of the research and agreed to contribute. On the whole groups willingly participated seeing this as a way of empowering the young people and enabling them to have a voice.

Within all the groups participants were given the opportunity to discuss their attitudes, knowledge and experiences of the PSNI, Police Ombudsman's Office and the Policing Board. Most of the discussion centred on the PSNI as the young people had more contact with them than the other policing organisations. The NISRA Omnibus survey (February 2002) found that 66% of 16-24 year olds were aware of the Police Ombudsman, an increase of 31% from the previous year. The Community Attitudes Survey (November 2001) revealed that 56% of 16-24 year olds had heard of the Policing Board and by April 2002 this had increased to 72%. The survey within this study (February 2003) indicated that 53% had heard of the Police Ombudsman's Office and 65% were aware of the Policing Board. The focus group discussions suggested that the extent of young people's knowledge of these bodies is extremely limited, exemplified by one female saying *'Oh, I have heard of them but what is it?' (Larne)*. Unsurprisingly, knowledge of and contact with the PSNI was common.

The following sections document the findings from both the qualitative and quantitative research. Section 3 provides an overview of the quantitative results, with the subsequent sections focusing on the various organisations. Section 4 focuses on the PSNI, Section 5 on the Police Ombudsman and Section 6 on the Policing Board.

3. Demographic Breakdown of Survey Respondents

This section documents the demographic findings of the survey. In total 1163 young people completed the survey between November 2002 and February 2003. The sample consisted of 554 males (48%) and 609 females (52%). Table 5 shows the number of people surveyed within each age category. Three people failed to complete this question.

Table 5 Age and gender split of participants

Age	Frequency	Percentage	Male		Female	
			Frequency	%	Frequency	%
Under 16	113	10	68	60	45	40
16-18	544	47	291	54	253	46
19-21	385	33	155	40	230	60
22-24	118	10	38	32	80	68
Total	1160	100	552	48	608	52
Missing	3	0.3	2		1	

Location

Postcodes were converted to District Command Units (DCUs), 25 of which correspond with District council areas. Belfast is divided into four areas (North, South, East and West). Table 6 shows the DCUs surveyed and the number of participants within each area. All 29 DCUs were represented.

The PSNI is organised into three geographical regions: Urban, North and South. Within these three areas 37% were surveyed in the Urban region (Greater Belfast, Antrim, Carrickfergus, Lisburn and the North Down area), 26% in the South Region (counties Tyrone, Armagh and Down) and 32% in the North Region (from Fermanagh in the west through to Derry Londonderry and across to Larne).

33

Table 6 DCUs surveyed

DCU	Frequency	Percentage
North Belfast	124	11
South Belfast	27	2
East Belfast	37	3
West Belfast	31	3
Antrim	27	2
Ards	46	4
Armagh	6	1
Ballymena	27	2
Ballymoney	21	2
Banbridge	10	1
Carrickfergus	11	1
Castlereagh	51	4
Coleraine	34	3
Cookstown	6	1
Craigavon	25	2
Down	135	12
Dungannon	30	3
Foyle	61	5
Fermanagh	89	8
Larne	20	2
Limavady	6	1
Lisburn	59	5
Magherafelt	11	1
Moyle	7	1
Newry and Mourne	40	3
Newtownabbey	74	6
North Down	49	4
Omagh	23	2
Strabane	13	1
Total	**1100**	**95**
Missing	63	5

Religious background

Of the 1163 people surveyed 567 (49%) considered themselves to be Catholic and 524 (45%) Protestant. These proportions correspond with the 2001 Census results, which reveal that 50% of 16-24 year olds identify themselves as Catholic and 46% as Protestant. Sixty-seven people (6%) considered themselves to be in the other category, these categories are displayed in Table 7. Other surveys have had a much higher proportion of Protestants to Catholics, McVeigh's (1994) study was based on 50% of Protestants, 31% Catholic and 19% others, while NISRA surveys have reported higher Protestant responses (56% compared to 39% Catholic).

Table 7 Religious background

Religion	Frequency
Catholic	567
Protestant	524
None	11
Atheist	8
Mixed (Protestant and Catholic)	7
Neither	6
Believe in God/Christian	3
Both (Protestant and Catholic)	2
Chinese	1
Chinese Buddhist	1
Chinese Mixed	1
Greek Orthodox	1
Indian	1
Jewish	1
Mixed Ethnic	1
Muslim	1
Non-denominational	1
Total	1137
Missing	26

Ethnic background

The majority of the sample (1134, 98%) classified themselves as having a white ethnic background, while 1% (13) was Chinese. The sample also included small numbers of individuals from other ethnic backgrounds (Table 8). This is broadly in line with the ethnic breakdown of the Northern Ireland population according to the data from the 2001 Census.

Table 8 Ethnic background

Ethnic background	Frequency	Percentage
White	1134	98
Chinese	13	1
Other	5	0.5
Mixed	3	0.5
Irish traveller	2	0.5
Black Caribbean	2	0.5
Indian	1	0.5
Total	1160	100
Missing	3	0.3

Education

The educational qualifications of participants are recorded in Table 9. The largest percentage of respondents are currently studying for or have achieved an HND/Degree or higher qualification.

Table 9 Educational qualification

Educational Qualification	Frequency	Percentage
None	100 46 (under) 16 54 (16+)	9 4 (under16) 5 (16+)
GCSEs	257	22
A-levels or equivalent	232	20
NVQ/BTEC	144	12
HND/Degree or Higher	409	35
Other	18	2
Total	1160	100
Missing	3	0.3

Crosstabulations

Crosstabulations were conducted in SPSS. Age, gender, location, community background and educational level were crosstabulated with the questions. These crosstabulations are referred to throughout the report.

4. The Police Service of Northern Ireland

4.1 Quantitative Findings

Young people's opinions about the police were ascertained as displayed in Table 10. Their opinions on and attitudes towards the police were mixed. More young people agreed than disagreed that the police were found to be honest, professional, helpful, there to protect them and acceptable. However, more disagreed than agreed that they were fair, able to understand youth issues, from their community or had improved since the organisation had changed from the RUC to the PSNI.

Table 10 Opinions about the PSNI

Statement	Percentage				
	Strongly Agree	Agree	Neither	Disagree	Strongly Disagree
I believe the police to be honest	6	31	33	20	11
I believe the police to be professional	7	40	28	19	6
I believe the police to be helpful	6	41	29	17	7
I believe the police to be fair	5	28	33	24	11
I believe the police to be there for my protection	13	41	24	15	8
I believe the police to be able to understand youth issues	6	25	33	25	12
I believe the police to be able to solve community problems	3	23	29	29	16
I believe the police to be acceptable	7	38	29	17	9
I believe the police to be from my community	4	21	35	23	17
I believe that policing has improved since becoming the PSNI	2	16	47	22	14

When these statements were crosstabulated with community background it was found that more Protestants than Catholics were inclined to either strongly agree or agree with the statements as shown in Table 11. However, fewer Protestants than Catholics felt that policing had improved since becoming the PSNI.

Table 11 Opinions about the PSNI according to community background

Statement	Percentage					
	Agree		Neither		Disagree	
Community Background	C	P	C	P	C	P
I believe the police to be honest	25	48	36	29	39	23
I believe the police to be professional	36	58	32	24	32	19
I believe the police to be helpful	40	55	33	24	27	21
I believe the police to be fair	22	44	35	29	43	27
I believe the police to be there for my protection	47	61	27	21	27	18
I believe the police to be able to understand youth issues	29	34	33	32	38	35
I believe the police to be able to solve community problems	23	31	27	31	50	39
I believe the police to be acceptable	35	55	33	26	33	19
I believe the police to be from my community	14	36	32	37	54	27
I believe that policing has improved since becoming the PSNI	23	12	44	47	33	41

When asked what main activities should the PSNI be concentrating on the top three were paramilitary activity (47%), drug dealing (45%) and assaults (40%), indicating some of the issues of concern to young people today. However, although drug dealing was a priority drug usage was not seen as being as important an issue, only 12% selected it in their top three (Table 12).

Table 12 Activities PSNI should be concentrating on

Activity	Frequency	Percentage
Paramilitary activity	546	47
Drug dealing	527	45
Assaults	470	40
Community safety	401	35
Crime prevention	356	31
Prompt response to emergencies	266	23
Car crime	245	21
Road safety	234	20
Drug use	134	12
Public disorder	122	11
Domestic burglary	105	9
Other	22	2

(participants were asked to select three)

Nearly half (45%) of the respondents had some form of contact with the police with 41% having had contact within the past 12 months. Males were found to have had more contact with the police than females (56% compared to 28% respectively). Those living in the urban region (51%) were also found to have more contact than those in either the south (41%) or north (31%) regions. In terms of educational qualification those with no formal qualifications were more likely to have contact with the PSNI (60%) compared to those within the HND/Degree or higher qualification bracket (32%). Community background did not affect levels of contact.

For the 45% (526 respondents) who had contact with the PSNI the nature of the contact varied (Table 13). Being stopped and questioned and being asked to move on were the two most frequently occurring forms of contact, especially for males. The focus group discussions revealed that most young people regard this form of contact as a form of harassment.

Table 13 What form did this contact take?

Nature of contact	Frequency	Percentage
Stopped and questioned	117	22
Asked to move on	103	20
Victim of crime	95	18
Other	74	14
Perpetrator of crime	69	13
Required to produce driving documents	61	12
Witnessed a crime	56	11

(participants were allowed to tick more than one)

The other forms of contact that were reported were extremely varied. They included contact through education, work, sport as well as a result of being involved in criminal activity and rioting. A full list of the various forms of contact that were described by respondents is detailed in Table 14.

Table 14 Other forms of contact respondents have had with the police

Contact	Frequency
Road traffic accident	6
Incidents at work and reporting crime	3
Was in a taxi that was stopped and asked to produce license	3
Talked to them	3
Questioned by the police	3
Community relations	3
Harassment	2
Hit with a plastic bullet	2
In my local area	2
Talking to them on the street on the way home at night	2
Witness to the scene of a crime/statement	2
Work placement in Ballymena Courthouse	2
Had to get police escort to local football match	2
Talk in school	2
Accused of a crime	2
Complaint about someone	1
Talked to them on work experience	1
Statement for claim	1
Arrested	1

Crashed into a police officer	1
House was searched	1
Give a statement	1
Rioting	1
Had abuse shouted at me	1
With a friend who was stopped and questioned	1
Participated in a community affairs forum	1
Lost purse	1
Signing up for identity parades- volunteer	1
Working in a partnership with street community level	1
To receive information on DAT 1 Form	1
Organise events that require police input	1
Needed police check to take place	1
Played hockey against them	1
Informed police of object on the M2 Motorway	1
Applied to do street collection	1
Member of the family	1
DNA testing for Baby Carrie	1
Police were trying to increase awareness as several break-in	1
Interviewed by them	1
Asked if I had witnessed a crime.	1
Because a burglar alarm was going off every night	1
Regarding a missing person	1
Family involvement in a supposed crime	1
Domestic	1
Needed help	1
Police Liaison meeting	1
Total	**71**
Missing	3

In terms of contact as a result of being a perpetrator of crime, more males than females (17% compared to only 6%) had police contact. Likewise those with no qualifications (40%) were more likely to have contact with police as perpetrators than individuals with higher qualifications such as HNDs and degrees (2%). Over half (64%) of the young people who had had contact with the PSNI said that this had taken place on the street, 18% said that it took place at their home while 6% said it occurred at school, college or work and a similar percentage noted that it had occurred at a police station or at a court.

Those who had contact with the PSNI were asked to indicate their level of satisfaction during the contact. Satisfaction varied as Table 15 illustrates. It was found that younger participants were more inclined to be dissatisfied, 31% of under 16s were very dissatisfied with the service compared to 13% of 19-21 year olds.

Table 15 Satisfaction with PSNI during contact

Satisfaction	Frequency	Percentage
Very satisfied	67	14
Satisfied	103	21
Neither satisfied nor dissatisfied	113	23
Dissatisfied	88	18
Very dissatisfied	115	24
Total	486	100

More than one in five young people (21%, 244 respondents) indicated that a police officer had behaved in an unacceptable way towards them. This is comparable to the findings of the recent PONI surveys (see Section 1.2). Younger participants and males were more likely to complain of unacceptable behaviour than older age ranges and females (46% of under 16's compared to 14% of 19-21 year olds and 33% of males compared to 10% of females). However community background did not seem to affect whether unacceptable behaviour was experienced or not, with 23% of Catholics and 20% of Protestants reporting unacceptable behaviour. Those within the urban region (32%) were more likely to report experiencing unacceptable behaviour than those in either the south (16%) or north regions (13%). Similarly more respondents in the urban region had made a complaint about police behaviour than elsewhere (8% compared to 2% (south region) and 4% (north region).

Of the 21% who reported unacceptable behaviour, 74% (179) had experienced such behaviour on three or less occasions (39% once, 24% twice and 11% three times). Thirty-six respondents (15%) reported experiencing unacceptable behaviour on four or more occasions. The types of behaviour experienced by this cohort are shown in Table 16. The largest percentage accused the police of being disrespectful or impolite of forms of verbal abuse. However more than one in four young people (27%) who reported unacceptable behaviour from a police officer said that the police had behaved in a violent manner.

Table 16 Types of unacceptable behaviour

Behaviour	Frequency	Percentage
Disrespectful or impolite	142	58
Swore	100	41
Wrongly accused of misbehaviour	93	38
Stopped or searched without reason	77	31
Harassment	71	29
Behaved in a violent way	66	27
Did not follow proper procedures	51	21
Did not carry out duty properly	39	16
Used sectarian, racist or sexist language	37	15
Took an item of property	31	12
Discrimination due to race, gender	16	6
Searched house without reason	11	4

(participants were allowed to tick more than one)

The younger age groups were more likely to report being wrongly accused of misbehaviour with over half of under 16 year olds (51%) compared to a quarter (25%) of 22-24 year olds. In addition females were less likely than males to experience violent behaviour (14% compared to 31%). Those within the Catholic community were more likely than those within the Protestant community to report disrespectful or impolite behaviour (65% compared to 50%) and the use of sectarian language (19% compared to 10%). However, Protestants felt that they were more likely to be harassed (32% compared to 26%) and wrongly accused of misbehaviour (43% compared to 34%) than Catholics.

Some 5% of all respondents (57 people), and 23% of those young people who had experience of unacceptable behaviour, had made a formal complaint about the police in the past 12 months, although in total 8% (94 respondents) had made a complaint at some stage. Community background did not affect whether or not a complaint had been made. Of the 8% who had complained one quarter (25%) had lodged their complaint at the local police station, 20% with a solicitor and 16% with the Police Ombudsman. Complaints against the police are dealt with in more detail in section 5.

4.2 Perceived Changes in Policing

The following sections focus on the qualitative findings of the research although the quantitative results are referred to where appropriate. This section discusses the perceived changes that have occurred within policing in Northern Ireland as a result of the reform initiated in response to the Patten Report and the change of name from the RUC to the PSNI in 2001.

In general, there was little or no difference between what Catholic and Protestant participants suggested. However, some Catholics made it clear that they felt that there had not been enough changes made or ground covered to build up trust within their community, while many Protestants felt that too many changes had been made. In both cases this served to undermine their trust in policing.

'I would be cautious, I wouldn't be trusting of them straight away' (Glengormley).

There was an overarching view within many of the groups that whatever changes had been made to policing *'it made no difference, it was all done for political reasons'*, while the notion that policing was highly politicised was of concern to a number of individuals who took part in the focus groups.

Physical and symbolic changes such as the name, badges and vehicles were referred to along with the appointment of a new chief constable, the disbandment of the band, the pledging of the royal oath. There was a limited knowledge of the changing structures of the police. Some participants suggested that there had been a change in the style of traffic vehicles, in the type of guns carried and in the amount of force used by officers, and in the frequency of arrests since the formation of the PSNI.

Police were regarded, with regret by most, to be less of a crime prevention organisation that provides a service to the community and more of a militia. The changes to the uniforms reinforced this 'swat' team notion. There were comments that the variety of uniforms caused confusion and some felt that the colours were meant to appeal more to one side than the other. A number of groups mentioned the martial design of the uniforms, especially the 'boiler suits', were perceived to be alienating and distancing. One person in the Omagh group felt that, *'Somebody's been watching too many US cop shows'*.

Some groups also discussed the policy of recruiting Protestants and Catholics in equal numbers. Most believed that more women and Catholics were now being welcomed and fewer Protestant males. A number of comments also noted that television and public advertisements had made a point of showing images of ethnic minorities in the new police organisation but their presence was not apparent in the service.

It is noteworthy that during these initial brainstorming sessions no mention was made of the Policing Board or the Police Ombudsman for Northern Ireland. This tendency to focus principally on changes, attitudes and experiences of PSNI was reflected throughout the discussions while a lack of familiarity necessitated that conversations were directed at the work of the DPPs, the Policing Board and Police Ombudsman to a much lesser extent.

Several young people acknowledged their own prejudices and biases in relation to the police, and admitted to difficulties in changing their views,

'I don't know, maybe it's just the way I've been brought up' (Belfast).

A number of those who were interviewed who were young offenders or were perceived to be at risk of offending, acknowledged their own negative behaviour to the police,

'oh aye we provoke them alright, but they don't acknowledge that they provoke us' (Hydebank).

The participants in this instance were drawing on their experiences of being persistently involved in rioting and other forms of anti-social behaviour, which brought them into frequent contact with the police. Participants in these focus groups were able to stimulate discussion between themselves that drew on comparative experiences with other police services in Great Britain and Ireland. However a sense that the police provoke young people was not exclusive to groups containing young offenders or those at risk of offending. In general there was an overriding sense from focus group participants that PSNI officers,

'think they're high and mighty, they can get off with everything' (Derry Londonderry).

This attitude could be interpreted as the railings of a disempowered social group who are confronted by a more powerful, self-reliant set of individuals, but the perceptions of the young people appears to greatly influence their confidence at engaging with or complaining about the police.

'I remember going to Londonderry for my best friend's hen night and there was three Land Rovers and all the police in riot gear and there was hardly a soul on the street before people came out of the nightclub. It was there to provoke, that's the way that I felt' (Derry Londonderry).

The alienation of young people from aspects of social and establishment authority, including the police, is a well-documented and researched phenomenon (Loader 1996, Hartless et al 1995, Ferrell 1995). In Northern Ireland these relationships are further problematised by the sectarian divisions and the security situation. It has been suggested that negative and anti-authoritarian perceptions are often formulated from an early age and these are in turn reinforced from within family and community (Connolly 2002). In other countries building relationships between the police and young people is done by a variety of means, including gathering information on individuals (Stol and Bervoets 2002), however in Northern Ireland this type of action is considered unwelcome and is perceived by some young people to be little more than low-level intelligence gathering exercises on the part of the security forces. This issue is discussed in more detail in relation to DPPs in Section 6.3.

4.3 Attitudes Towards the PSNI

Participants in all focus groups agreed that a democratic society should have a statutory police service. Many participants wanted the service to be a more 'civil' citizen-based service rather than an organisation that was there simply to apprehend perpetrators.

'The organisation is meant to be there to protect and serve the public, whether they do it or not is debatable' (Fermanagh).

In general, the young people's principal concerns were with the quality of the personal contacts they had with individuals in the police. Many wished for a policing service in which all citizens could be confident, but they felt that this was a long-term goal and not one that was easily achievable.

Sixteen participants disclosed that they had family members who had served within the RUC, but less than five focus group participants acknowledged having family members as serving PSNI officers. Those who disclosed these relationships were often keen to distance themselves from the serving family members,

'my cousin is a disaster, he'd book his granny, he's aiming for up the ladder' (Omagh).

In groups where personal information and emotions were more frankly exchanged, sympathy for and empathy with the families of police officers were frequently demonstrated,

'I know what it's like my Dad was in the UDR, it wasn't nice waiting for him to come home …. where I live they have to know where we are and what we're doing for safety reasons and you still have to check your car for bombs' (Fermanagh).

The disclosures of such confidences would often stimulate more revealing discussions within the groups. However overall there was a clearly articulated lack of awareness of, or curiosity in, the process and procedures of policing, which they felt was alien to their short-term interests. While the groups who participated in the research welcomed the opportunity to influence policing policy, many doubted whether their views, recommendations and wishes would lead to any significant change. The dominant perception was that consultation with young people was not principally for the benefit of the young people, for whom policing issues were not a central or daily concern, rather, they saw their participation as an exercise in tokenism. They were also keen that this opinion should be reflected within the report.

Joining the Police?

'There should be a police service, but I don't want to get involved' (Craigavon).

The questionnaire revealed that only 17% (197 respondents) would or had considered joining the police, with fewer Catholics (11%) than Protestants (23%) having considered the option. When asked why they would not consider joining the main reason given was safety, with 36% fearing the possibility of attack on their family and 35% fearing attack on themselves. The fear of attack on families was higher among the Catholic community (42% compared to 31% within the Protestant community) and was also slightly higher in terms of individual attack (39% within the Catholic community compared to 32% within the Protestant community).

Nearly one third (32%) indicated that they did not support the police and therefore would have no desire to join. This lack of support was higher among the Catholic community (38%) than the Protestant community (27%) (Figure 1). The main reason cited within the other category (16%) was that joining the police did not fit into the overall career plans chosen. This was also discussed within the focus group sessions with many participants feeling that their lack of interest in joining the police should not focus predominantly on factors related to the police, but rather on their interest in other careers. Those who indicated an interest in pursuing careers related to civil rights and responsibilities felt that there were jobs within other organisations that would be less politicised and controversial.

Figure 1 Level of support for the police according to community background

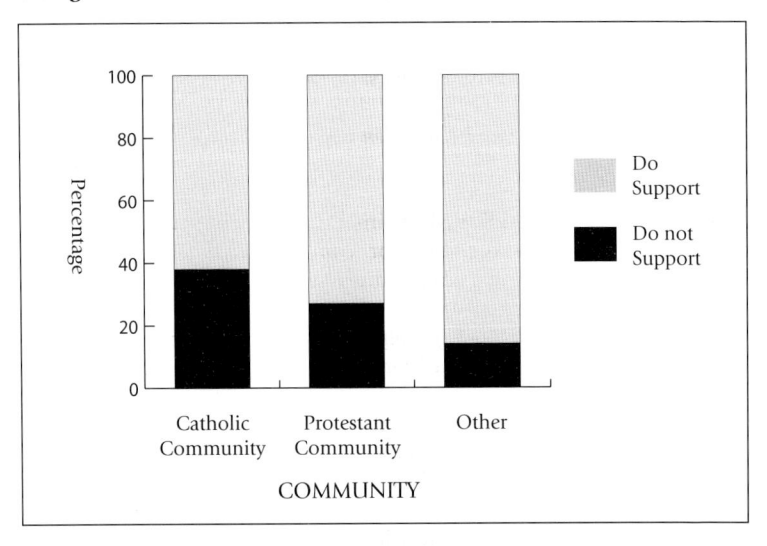

[Bar chart showing percentage of Do Support and Do Not Support across Catholic Community, Protestant Community, and Other. Catholic Community shows approximately 38% Do Not Support; Protestant Community shows approximately 27% Do Not Support; Other shows approximately 15% Do Not Support.]

The politicised nature of any business surrounding the work of the PSNI was often the reason cited for pressure being put on individuals from family, friends and the wider community to pursue a career other than policing. A wide range of respondents, Catholic and Protestant, male and female, also said that a lack of respect for the organisation from their communities would also affect their decisions. Furthermore, there was concern from within a number of working-class Protestant estates that members of paramilitary organisations in the area used pernicious ways to discourage people from joining by intimidating families of officers,

'They would do your ma or da and put them out' (Belfast).

'They're spraying registrations of vehicles on the walls in Rathcoole now' (Belfast).

For both Catholics and Protestants, there was an issue around the safety of their family and friends and in addition, they believed that there would be a reduced opportunity to socialise in their home areas and with whom they wanted to.

In general young Protestant men and women demonstrated more willingness to join but because of the current recruitment policies they felt they were less likely to be chosen,

'my mother said 'no offence, but you won't be accepted, you're the wrong religion'(Belfast),

while a Protestant male from Belfast suggested that,

'Protestants now feel intimidated and don't apply – we should complain about that' (Belfast).

Those Catholics who indicated an interest in joining were frequently discouraged by family members or community/peer pressure. One woman from a strong republican family background said,

'my daddy wouldn't speak to me if I joined, when the advert came on the telly I said to him that I might join and he said don't even think about it' (Belfast).

Similarly, a respondent from a nationalist estate in Belfast, whose decision to join was initially supported by the family, was dissuaded by a grandparent who said *'you won't be able to live here.'*

There was also a concern that the selection and recruitment process was not sufficiently accountable to applicants. One Catholic male had been turned down and felt the lack of transparency in the process did not encourage people to apply,

'I didn't get past the third stage and I would have liked some feedback why not' (Derry Londonderry)

Some participants were deterred from joining the police because of factors relating directly to the day to day working of the organisation.

Frequently cited reasons for their reluctance to join PSNI included the unsociable hours, the working environment, and a preconception that,

'it's kind of a man's job, when you hear a man's roar people stop, but women don't have that strength' (Fermanagh female).

This type of gender bias from within the community was noted in other rural areas, for example in Omagh two women were discouraged from applying due to their gender. In general the police service was considered as a patriarchal institution and not an appropriate career for young women.

Mediated Views

The media was acknowledged to play a powerful and influential role in the representation of the police and thus to affect young people's perceptions of the organisation and its work. Some groups who had recounted positive personal experiences of the police felt their opinions had subsequently been clouded by the media focusing on other people's bad experiences. The BBC NI programme *South City Beat* was remembered in one Omagh group because of the comments of one WPC about her regulation boots, *'you could give someone a good kicking with those.'* The group, who were fundamentally supportive of the police, suggested that this should be addressed and countered by a media and publicity campaign on behalf of the police service rather than passively accepting that the police will get a bad press all the time.

4.4 Experiences of policing

In the focus groups some participants recounted incidents with the police that were second-hand and had in turn become highly coloured, even mythologised, in the telling and re-telling. Knowledge of these episodes had become part of a collective local memory and such incidents were often reinforced both inside the home and within the wider residential community. These narratives stimulated debate within the group, and although the details of the experiences have not been included in the report, their legacy of impressions and assumptions have impacted upon the perspectives that young people have of the police.

The focus group discussions indicated that the young people's experiences of the police in Northern Ireland have not altered since the service became the PSNI. One young male did however comment that he felt that there was a change in how they reacted to young people *'they are certainly more friendly, they now talk to me'*. While a group of males in Newtownabbey said that they felt *'sorry for the police'* as

'they are hit by all sides, the Catholics, the Protestants and now that woman (Police Ombudsman)' (Monkstown).

Others were adamant that in spite of the changes, their experiences of the police had not altered and these still were predominantly negative. At times the researchers perceived that the young people felt that they had to display a rebellious and anti-authoritarian stance against the police, as this was what was expected of them in spite of their experiences. Within one group a young male said,

'You know there are some good cops and they aren't all bad' (Belfast).

However, in spite of this recognition his opinions were predominantly negative, a reflection of his personal experiences. Personal experiences of the police have left many individuals with an over-riding feeling of being humiliated and harassed, and with a lack of trust in the organisation. This was heightened by a sense that the police put their own safety over that of citizens in potentially dangerous situations,

'they don't want to get involved, they just sit and watch' (Ballymena).

Young people's perceptions of the PSNI were dependent on the circumstances of contact. Some of the older participants described how their experiences whilst in work were different from when they were walking down the street,

'I am treated with respect at (place of work) but when I walk down the street in the estate I am harassed' (Belfast).

This individual felt that he couldn't challenge this change in attitude and he questioned the reasons for the change of treatment. He concluded that the differing treatment was because of the area in which he lived and not due to his behaviour as an individual. However, others felt that they were constantly being harassed at home and at work,

'They stop me coming in and out of work all the time' (Belfast).

This perception of constant harassment had led this young person to dislike the police. Likewise another individual said that he was *'stopped loads of times'* when he drives his girlfriend home, but the car is never stopped when his father drives it. This male said that young people often felt they had to prove their innocence, *'you're guilty until you can prove you are innocent' (Downpatrick).* However, some of the young people had more positive contact with the police and therefore more positive experiences,

'they came into our school and talked to us ... they seemed dead on' (Ballymena).

One female stated that the police had only ever been helpful to her, *'I broke down in my car and they stopped to help – that has always been my experience' (Larne).*

This young person had never encountered the police in a negative way and throughout the discussion was positive and enthusiastic about the service. Likewise another female who had encountered the police through her work described them as *'courteous and helpful'*.

Service or Intrusion?

Many of the groups felt that the police presence in their area had increased in recent times. Some groups viewed this as *'a way to crack down on crime'*, this was especially noted in areas of political violence such as the interface communities. One group stated that *'they're everywhere now'* attributing this to the rioting around areas in North Belfast. Others felt that an increased presence would only contribute to problems in their area,

'they are always here and it just entices people into a riot as they come in too heavy handed' (Belfast).

For some young people who did not live in areas with high levels of political violence, there was a degree of sympathy for the police who they felt were caught between the two sides. In other areas, especially rural districts, the policing presence was perceived as having been scaled down and therefore contact with them was limited,

'There's only two in (name of village) so we don't use them anyway' (Derry Londonderry).

In Omagh one group suggested there were 'less on the road' and attributed this to a reduction of the large police presence in the area after the bomb of 1998. A group from the Waterside (Derry Londonderry) suggested *'you never see them in the area unless there's a march'.* Similarly, a Ballymena group attributed an increased police presence with a seasonal (Christmas) preoccupation with drink drivers.

For some young people the primary nature of their contact with the police was through some form of surveillance. This was considered a violation of privacy or as an intrusive intelligence gathering exercise and was of concern to the majority of focus group participants. Many commented on the installation of CCTV cameras, to an increase in the use of still cameras by officers, in particular from vehicles and the perceived increase use of jeeps fitted with surveillance material,

'They've got cameras on the top of them (Belfast).'

In addition to issues of privacy, the methods of surveillance were also a matter of concern as an example of how participants felt the PSNI demonstrated insensitivity to the lives of citizens: *'They're all perverts, taking pictures all the time'* (Belfast).

This, some individuals felt, could be demonstrated in a number of contexts but in particular by the prevalent use of unmarked cars for surveillance purposes. Women from one Belfast-based group felt that particularly in the light of the loyalist feud, being followed in an unmarked car *'was a very scary experience'.*

Although one focus group in Newry felt that the changes in policing were positive, and had led to a better form of service and a more rapid response rate than before, it was more usual to note complaints in relation to police responses to problems,

'There was a big fight in the street and the police were called they didn't come for about an hour and a half by then it was all over' (Belfast),

'They are slow to respond I feel less secure because of this' (Glengormley).

Of particular concern was the threat of or actual domestic violence, which was mentioned in a number of sessions. Members of a Glengormley group suggested that repeated slow responses to domestic situations result in a lack of confidence, particularly from women and those who perceive themselves to be vulnerable. Furthermore the Newry group, which had indicated the most positive feedback on the response rate, also suggested that police had a different attitude and were slower to respond to incidents where domestic violence was the cause *'they don't come out quick enough for domestics'*.

There was a perception that police resources were always available to respond to riot situations but were rarely available for 'ordinary' policing problems and were particularly poor in situations involving domestic violence, which left women and children at risk.

Two other matters where response times were specifically mentioned were in relation to those living in rural areas and in incidents where fingerprint specialists were involved. A number of participants, in Downpatrick, Dungiven and Fermanagh, commented that the PSNI serviced the community badly by having rural area police stations only open part time and with a low-staffing ratio. This was not just of concern in matters of safety and security, but also informed how the young people perceived the police to treat them with a degree of casualness,

'I witnessed a car accident, it was a drunk driver and the police told us to go to the barracks next day which was about 16 mile away. It was a waste of time because the boy wasn't there so we had to return home again after walking all the way there and there was a closer police barracks than that one we could have gone to' (Omagh).

A number of participants also commented on the slow response time by fingerprints specialists,

'They have unreasonable expectations of how long you can wait for finger printers to come out, it can be up to a week' (Glengormley).

The slow process for this particular practice seemed to indicate that the police were not expecting their investigations to lead to arrests or else they would ensure that finger printing was carried out more rapidly, in particular in situations such as car thefts or domestic burglaries where it was impractical to wait in excess of 12 hours.

In addressing their attitudes towards the PSNI many participants acknowledged that their perception was based on a feeling that the police appeared to focus their attention on paramilitary and civil disturbances rather than on community issues *'they should get back to community things'*. A number of groups that were exclusively female or had women participants also commented on the fact that changes within the PSNI did not address issues of community safety and public service that were of particular concern to women.

Policing Young People

Some younger participants expressed frustration that it was always assumed by the PSNI (and adults) that they were *'up to no good'*,

'we were messing about playing football and the ball got stuck on the roof of the church. So we had to try and get up to get the ball ... this guy spotted us ... within minutes the police were there ... and we were trying to get away without getting caught as they would think we were up to no good' (Monkstown).

It was also felt that adults within the area exacerbated the situation and simply 'hanging about' gave some people cause for complaint,

'we were in my garden playing football and (name of neighbour) complained and they (the police) came and said 'is there any chance of all you moving' (Monkstown).

Some participants recognised that sometimes they were in the wrong and that the police were justified but thought that on other occasions they were not given the opportunity to explain either their version of events or how they felt about the situation,

'they actually don't listen to you right. Fair enough, sometimes you're in the wrong but sometimes they don't let you explain. It's more like you are in the wrong now listen to my lecture that's what they're like, they just like to talk away and slabber. Like you get the odd cop who would listen to you and he understands if you know what I mean' (Monkstown).

It was also felt that police attitudes towards young people differed from those held for adults and that *'the police don't take youths seriously'*. One young male participant said that when he went to report an attack on his car the incident was not taken seriously until his father arrived,

'they said 'what do you want us to do about it?', but their attitude changed when my dad came in' (Glengormley).

This annoyed the youth who said he felt that he was not considered *'important enough'* to listen to. Another young male who had gone out of his way to report a faulty railway barrier and ringing alarm also reported a similar experience. The young man said that he left the station feeling *'foolish'*,

'I came out of the station and thought what was the point of that' (Craigavon).

He also said that he felt that an adult would have been treated very differently. The experiences and perception among young people that the police treat them differently and in a specific manner because they are young was strong. Young people felt that police officers believed they could treat them as they wished and with little consideration or respect because there was a widely held view that groups of young people hanging around equals trouble. This perception was widespread among young people from a variety of backgrounds and in particular among young people from working class areas.

Protestant or Catholic?

Experiences did not vastly differ within the various communities and both Protestant and Catholic young people felt that the police 'were always on their case'. However, each side felt that their community was the one that suffered the most,

'Protestants get less hassle' (Belfast),

'They just back the ones on the other side (Protestants) they are their mates' (Belfast),

'Catholics get an easier time as they are feared of them' (Belfast).

Ellison (2001) found that more young Catholics than young Protestants construed that negative encounters with a police officer constituted a form of harassment, but that similar proportions had been told off, told to move on, questioned or searched by the police. However, within this research the context of the 'hassle' varied. Protestants felt that they received more hassle at parades whereas Catholics felt they were subjected to more hassle or 'picked upon' during a riot situation.

Males who had contact with the PSNI through riot situations or who came from communities that were highly politicised irrespective of any police contact, felt that they were targeted by police because of their perceived religious/sectarian backgrounds. Protestant males assumed that they were 'picked on' because they were Protestant, and were assumed to be loyalists: *'They're scared of the Catholics'*, suggested one Belfast-based Protestant focus group. Members of this group also perceived the pro-Catholic recruitment of new officers to be discrimination against Protestants and felt that the changes within the police had been carried out just to please Catholics, *'there was no need to change the name, only because the Catholics had wanted it' (Belfast).*

A similar attitude was held by youths from predominantly nationalist areas, who believed that police officers discriminated in favour of Protestants, *'If you're wearing a poppy you won't get stopped' (Fermanagh).* It was also felt that the reform of the police had been limited by unionist pressure,

'There's been no difference and no point in the changes, it's just not relevant, it was done to suit the unionists' (Belfast).

Concerns were also articulated that while some changes had taken place, new police officers were quickly institutionalised into an intrinsically biased organisation. The fear was expressed that while a sectarian balance in the recruitment process is being addressed, the views and attitudes of police officers may remain unchanged,

'an older cop and his views from old RUC days will influence the younger cop' (Belfast).

This attitude illustrates the significance that many give to police culture, but also demonstrates a tendency for many participants to depersonalise officers and to render them devoid of any individuality, and to see them simply as representatives of an institution.

Young and Chinese

The experiences of the PSNI of young people from within the Chinese community were not significantly different from any other young people's group participating in the research. Similar dissatisfactions were noted with the perceived slow response times of the police and of being told to 'move on' when hanging around in public places. The group did however complain that ethnic minorities were rarely represented within the PSNI and this was something that they would like to see changed.

Class Matters

The broad similarities in perspectives among young people from within different communities lends support to the contention of one focus group of young men in South Belfast. They disputed that religion had any effect on their experiences with the police and instead argued that more negative experiences were related to class background and socio-economic grouping rather than to ethno-religious background,

'It is as if they think working class have less power ... working class communities are treated differently ... someone walking down the street in a working class community will be stopped but not in middle class area' (Belfast).

Research has indicated that young people from socio-economically disadvantaged areas are over twice as likely to have been searched by a police officer and have experienced more police instigated encounters than young people from affluent neighbourhoods (Ellison 2001). McVeigh (1994) also found that while people explain harassment in sectarian or gender terms there is a strong correlation between working class and being harassed.

Male or Female?

The experiences of males and females were perceived by males to differ, with males feeling that females were not as harshly treated, *'they discriminate against boys'.* It was also felt that in Belfast city centre females had more freedom,

'If females are standing together they are less likely to be told to move on' (Belfast).

Ellison (2001) also found that females were less likely to be 'told off' or 'told to move on'. However, one young female from Derry Londonderry, who had had several encounters with the police, disagreed and said that she had been a victim of police brutality and that being female was no different. Another young woman from Belfast said that being female did not stop her from 'getting jumped'. It is however, perceived that young females have lower levels of adversarial contact with the police as they are not stereotyped (to the same extent) by the police or adults as 'trouble' (Anderson et al, 1994).

Being Harassed

The young people involved in the focus groups raised a number of issues that were of concern to them and which were a consequence of their perception that the police reacted and responded differently to them because they were young. Many of the issues can be broadly grouped under the heading of harassment, although harassment was experienced and perceived in many forms.

Harassment can be difficult to define as what one individual may perceive as harassment another may not. McVeigh (1994) emphasised that 'harassment means different things to different people'. In this research no singular or overarching definition of what constituted harassment was established, for some harassment was viewed as the mere presence of police officers, while for others it required some form of physical or verbal contact.

The nature of harassment as 'the use and abuse of power' (McVeigh, 1994) is how many young people view their experiences with the police. Ellison (2001) found that Catholic males were more likely than Protestant males to construe police instigated encounters as 'harassment', irrespective of the circumstances in which it took place. He also noted that the police officers themselves considered their behaviour as merely an everyday aspect of their work. McVeigh (1994) found that over one quarter of all young people in Northern Ireland felt that the security forces had harassed them. The young people in this research identified a variety of forms of police behaviour that they considered constituted harassment.

Physical Violence

Some of the young people stated that they had either been subjected to or witnessed police brutality,

'I saw a person getting a kicking from the peelers once right at the side of the chippy it was out in the street too. He started slabbering back and they got his head and hit it off the wall' (Monkstown).

Other examples of brutality included being thrown about the cell or police van, rough handling when putting on hand cuffs and putting these on to ensure they *'cut into your wrists if you move in a certain way' (Hydebank)*. This behaviour was widely condemned but was also accepted as being *'the way they (the police) operate'.*

This culture of physical violence and brutality has been accepted in Northern Ireland, and other violently divided societies, with young people perceiving it as normal behaviour (Smyth et al, 2002). Physical violence was the behaviour that most people felt would give them the right to complain, *'I would complain if they hit me or done something to me' (Belfast)*. While such behaviour would be widely condemned it was only the most extreme of a variety of forms of harassment that young people described.

A Constant Presence

Many of the participants felt that as young people they encountered frequent harassment and simply had to put up with being picked upon. One group of Protestants in a loyalist area of Belfast summed up how they felt,

'they are aggressive, intrusive, in your face, condescending and generally ignorant' (Belfast).

This view was expressed not only by those who had been in trouble but also by young people who had witnessed the harassment of others. For some of the older participants this harassment was evident at nightclubs where the view was that a constant police presence enticed trouble,

'You always have run ins when you are out on a night out through the weekend ... they are always standing at night clubs in case there is any bother ... and just entice people to start' (Ballymena).

This harassment of young people was even more evident if they were affected by alcohol,

'They treat you like scum because you have a drink in you' (Ballymena).

The young people who felt that the police were constantly harassing them had mainly negative opinions and stated that the seemingly constant presence of the police was a source of irritation.

Confiscating Goods

Some young people complained that items in their possession would be confiscated, and this was viewed as a form of harassment. One individual complained that he had his alcohol confiscated,

'I have had drink taken off me – just carrying it from one house to the other'

Researcher: *What age are you?*

'Under 18, but they didn't know that at the time' (Monkstown).

In situations like this some of the young people interviewed recognised that they may have been in the wrong and that police action was required, however this young male felt that in this case their action had not been justified.

A young female from Belfast also complained to the researchers that she had her bike taken from her for finger printing and three years on *'they're still taking fingerprints'*. This young woman felt that she would never get her bike back in spite of the fact that she had been to the police station to complain about the delays.

Being Watched

Some young people complained of being constantly followed, especially if they were driving. In some areas the young people were also convinced that they were being photographed secretly,

'The cameras hidden (name of building) are constantly pointing at this estate and are constantly taking photographs' (Belfast).

Such activities made the individuals feel humiliated,

'You feel like a wee boy … it makes you feel that you are doing something wrong and others who see you being hassled think 'he must be a bad one' (Belfast).

One young man felt that if he was going to be harassed for doing nothing he might as well do something to make the harassment worthwhile. Those who had encountered such harassment were quick to point out that not all the 'peelers' were guilty and that in most cases it would be either one or two individuals,

'Most of the times I've got stopped it has always been the same peeler so it has, he always, always harasses me' (Belfast).

Verbal Abuse

Some participants complained that they endured a variety of types of verbal abuse from members of the PSNI, this mainly took the form of name-calling and offensive joking. One young male said that he was picked upon because of his prominent front teeth,

'Slagging my teeth and saying Donkey Mouth … sticking their teeth out the window and all' (Dungannon).

The adult who facilitated this group revealed that he had heard this individual being verbally abused and had challenged the policeman in question but he had not been satisfied with the response. Another individual said, *'they make jokes about people and they'll try to aggravate you with comments about people you know, and even make offensive comments about your family, they'll talk about them and pick on them ... my cousin they call him big ears in the middle of the street – it's embarrassing for him' (Portadown).*

Some of the participants acknowledged that the verbal abuse they had received was in many ways justified, as it was in response to them 'slabbering' at the police in the first instance. This in turn suggests something of a process whereby each group feels it is acceptable to verbally abuse the other. However any suggestion that this makes things equal does not acknowledge that verbal harassment is but one form of a complex range of behaviours that are considered offensive and abuse of power by young people.

4.4 Power, Authority and Age

It is evident from the research that young people hold a variety of preconceptions about the police and they believe the police hold similar preconceptions about young people. These recurring assumptions were not related to the participants' age, gender, social class or religious affiliation. In general, young people stated that they did not feel supported by figures of authority and often felt disenfranchised, vulnerable and powerless.

Awareness of power imbalances in their social relationships due to their age was a concern for many young people. They appeared to be acutely disturbed by the fact that they were peripheral to any decision-making within communities and this general tendency was particularly apparent in their dealings with policing organisations. They claimed to feel vulnerable and were unable to challenge attitudes that they found unacceptable and unwelcome from within the police service. It was claimed that many officers behaved in a way that was 'less than human' and didn't display any respect for young people.

A number of respondents, in particular young offenders or those at risk of offending, felt socially isolated in their communities and articulated a feeling of harassment by the police. Some of those referred to themselves as 'hoods' (young criminals with no paramilitary connections) commented that in their communities, support for the statutory policing service was not forthcoming and instead alternative forms of policing were being experimented with. Consequently community representatives and paramilitary 'big men' were the primary source of authority for many in the neighbourhoods and the 'hoods' felt that they fell between two stools, *'We have no power, we can't turn anywhere'*. They felt doubly socially isolated, intimidated and under physical threat from both the police service and from the perceived community representatives. Both groups, they suggested, were equally intolerant of anti-social behaviour and were likely to judge individuals by the lack of support for their organisation as much as by their actions.

There was general support among young people for restorative justice programmes. Participants see them as serving a dual purpose, protecting them both from paramilitary attack and from engagement with statutory policing and ultimately the judicial system. Participation in these programmes is also seen to be likely to provide material rewards by enabling the offenders to access agencies, which could prioritise and support their individual social needs,

'you're more likely to get a house quick with Base 2 if you're on the Alternatives programme' (Hydebank).

In many areas, statutory policing was less favoured than paramilitary policing because the young people perceived there would be different, and more responsive engagement at an individual level. Police officers were generally thought to be unsympathetic to their position and feelings of anger, humiliation and embarrassment were frequently acknowledged as the key emotions connected to engaging with the police,

'the police have it in for me, it does your head in' (Dungannon).

Some groups with members from loyalist (N=5) and republican communities (N=7) demonstrated more confidence in the immediacy and effectiveness of the paramilitaries response than to that of the police,

'We don't need the RUC – the community has got its own helpers and they do more, when the alarm goes off, we know the Taigs have started' (Belfast)

'We know who to turn to in the community to get things done, we just go up to the Sinn Fein centre and they pass it on' (Derry Londonderry).

The confidence that the paramilitary organisations will provide a better form of 'policing' or support appears to be influenced by a lack of confidence in statutory policing. It is also affected by a concern that calling in the police rather than utilising 'informal' policing services could be looked upon badly by powerful people within the community and this in turn could be harmful to individuals and their families

'they'd do your ma and da and put them out' (Belfast).

Members of many focus groups expressed a belief that it was unlikely that they would be able to build positive relationships with the police and policing agencies because of a lack of 'proper, fair policing'. However they felt that all parties should try to develop a mutual understanding of each others positions including looking at stereotyping, provocative behaviour and human respect on the part of the police, the young people and community representatives with the aim of building up confidence.

5. Police Ombudsman for Northern Ireland

5.1 Quantitative Findings

Fifty-seven people who completed the questionnaire (5% of the sample) said they had made a complaint about the police in the past 12 months (although 94 respondents (8% of the sample) said they had made a formal complaint about police behaviour at some stage). This number represents just over 23% of those people who reported that they had experienced unacceptable behaviour from the police. While this is a relatively low figure, it is however slightly higher than the findings of the recent PONI surveys. These have indicated that around 17% of people who had experienced unacceptable behaviour had lodged a formal complaint (see Section 1.2). Table 17 shows where complaints had been lodged by the complainants.

Table 17 Organisation where complaint was lodged

Organisation	Frequency	Percentage
Local Police Station	24	26
Solicitor	19	20
Police Ombudsman	15	16
Chief Constable	4	4
MP/MLA/Councillor	4	4
Other	2	2
Did not know who to complain to	2	2
Did not know how to complain	1	1
Don't know	1	1
CAB	0	0

(participants were allowed to tick more than one, some participants who had made a complaint did not respond to this question)

Over half (52%) of respondents had heard of the Police Ombudsman's Office with awareness being greater among older participants (72% of 22-24 year olds were aware of the Police Ombudsman compared to only 27% of under 16s) and those within the higher education brackets (70% with an HND or degree compared to 33% who had no formal qualification). Awareness had mainly come through television (40%) and the focus group discussions also revealed that the media reports concerning the Omagh bomb investigation had increased young people's awareness.

Nearly three quarters (72%) of those who had heard of the Police Ombudsman recognised her role as being 'to investigate complaints against the police'. Table 18 shows the responses received.

Table 18 What do you think the role of the Police Ombudsman is?

Role	Frequency	Percentage
To investigate complaints against the police	494	72
To receive complaints	173	25
Don't know	83	12
To investigate complaints by the police	67	10
To protect the police from investigation	21	3

(participants were allowed to tick more than one)

Only 11% of the respondents (130 people) said they knew how to contact the Police Ombudsman if they had a complaint concerning the PSNI with only 2% (24 people) ever having contacted the Office directly.

Just over one quarter (26%) of those who had made a complaint to any of the relevant bodies said that they were happy with the service they had received. Three main reasons were cited by those who were unhappy with the service they had received:
- the process took too long (21%);
- the complaint was not taken seriously and (21%);
- the complainant did not hear anything after making the complaint (21%).

Slightly more people were happy with the service they had received from the Police Ombudsman: 38% (8 people) said they were happy with the service. Three people omitted to answer whether or not they were happy with the service. Of the 62% (13 people) who were not happy with the service the two main reasons given for their dissatisfaction were:
- a slow response (33%);
- the feeling that their complaint was not taken seriously (33%).

This feeling was echoed in the discussion groups where young people felt that their complaint would not be taken seriously and therefore were discouraged from complaining formally. Also for the 33% who had a complaint but chose not to complain 59% felt that the police would not do anything therefore their efforts would be wasted.

The series of questions regarding opinions of the Police Ombudsman show that the majority of respondents opted for the neither agree nor disagree option. Table 19 illustrates the responses given to the questions and between 23% and 47% agreed or strongly agreed with the various statements viewing the Police Ombudsman's Office in a positive way. When these responses were crosstabulated with community background few differences were noted between Catholics and Protestants. However, one exception was noted with more Catholics agreeing that the Police Ombudsman was necessary (57% compared to 43% among the Protestant community).

Table 19 Opinions about the Police Ombudsman

Statement	Strongly Agree	Agree	Neither	Disagree	Strongly Disagree
Police Ombudsman will help Police do a better job	4	28	49	9	3
Police Ombudsman is impartial	3	20	58	9	4
Police Ombudsman is independent of the police	4	24	55	9	3
Police Ombudsman treats a person complaining fairly	3	24	58	6	3
Police Ombudsman investigates complaints against the police fairly	3	22	58	9	3
Police Ombudsman is necessary	18	29	42	3	3
Police Ombudsman can help change the police and make it more acceptable	6	27	51	7	4

5.2 Attitudes and Knowledge of Police Ombudsman

The Police Ombudsman's Office was not considered to be easily accessible and for those people living outside Belfast it was felt that it *'was bound to be Belfast-based'*. Some were aware of the organisation and the gender of the Police Ombudsman with a few aware of her name, *'Nuala Pot Noodle?'* cracked one person. Some were unclear about the role and work of the Office, although 72% in the survey had a clear indication of her role defining it as *'investigating complaints against the police'*. Knowledge centred on the basis of highly publicised events,

'Isn't she something to do with the police and the Omagh bomb?' *(Monkstown).*

One young woman who worked in the Citizens' Advice Bureau told her group that the Police Ombudsman's Office was impartial and,

'if you have a complaint they look into it ... they use our Offices for interviews' *(Omagh).*

However, none of the other group members were aware that this was the case, and none of the young people who had made a complaint against the police had done it through a Citizen's Advice Bureau (Table 17). This highlights a basic lack of knowledge of the Police Ombudsman's operations and procedures even if there is a general awareness of the office and of its role. There was also a belief that attempting to use the Office as part of the process of rebuilding confidence in the police was flawed,

'There's been such a history of abuse to both Catholics and Protestants from the police that it will take more to correct this than setting up an Ombudsman's Office.' (Glengormley).

Those who did know about the Police Ombudsman's Office frequently assumed that it was there to 'Police the Police' and when they were more familiar with the role there was a degree of scepticism about its impartiality and efficacy,

'It's pointless to complain, no-one will listen, it's their word against mine' *(Belfast).*

However, the survey indicated that the Police Ombudsman's Office is generally viewed in a positive way as shown in Table 19. Some within the focus groups who knew of the Office did however feel that there was an inbuilt relationship between the police and the Ombudsman and this in turn led to a lack of trust within the system,

'you wouldn't feel safe giving details, you don't know who would get hold of it' *(Hazelwood).*

'I wouldn't trust information as being safe' (Hazelwood).

'It would be my word against theirs' (Glengormley).

'They'd just stick up for their colleagues' (Belfast).

'The courts will always believe the Police'(Belfast).

In addition, the lack of impartiality was compounded by a fundamental belief among some young people of collusion between the police and loyalists, which would have implications particularly for those within nationalist and loyalist communities. Many therefore felt there would be little point in making any complaints and the police's position over minor complaints would stand,

'they would only say there were sitting outside your house reading a paper or doing normal checks' (Belfast).

For those who were familiar with the aims of the Police Ombudsman, there was a degree of scepticism about the Office's accountability. A number of positive suggestions were made to enable the Office to be seen to be more transparent. These will be considered more fully in Section 7, but they included suggestions that there should be *'more feedback' (Portadown)*, and that the Office *'should ensure people know when police officers are reprimanded' (Hydebank)*.

While many understood the organisation to be a separate body to the PSNI, the incorporation of the name Police into the Ombudsman's title undermined its perceived impartiality. This concern was compounded by the expectation of some that people working at the Police Ombudsman's Office would be former police officers or people who have worked in law enforcement. It was felt that the 'set a thief to catch a thief' attitude was not without complications in the form of built-in prejudices and biases.

5.3 Experiences of the Police Ombudsman

As has already been noted some people had a basic knowledge of the Police Ombudsman's Office while those who had made a complaint about the police (either current or past) had a greater knowledge. The experiences that were expressed were based on either actual or perceived knowledge of the Office and of the handling of a complaint. Much of the discussion concerning experiences was also based upon the Omagh bomb investigation – for many this was the first time they had heard of the Police Ombudsman's Office. A number of leading news items in the days prior to focus groups being conducted often reflected the participants' only understanding of the organisations. For the Office, Omagh was a frequently cited instance, though many had heard the name they had not absorbed the information in the news bulletins. Subsequently, their acquaintance with these bodies was scant and while the name was recognised there was no deeper knowledge. In fact young people's knowledge and insight into the workings of such public bodies was minimal and frequently non-existent. What limited knowledge there was frequently proved to be inaccurate. Comments such as *'Aren't they something to do with the marches?* (Larne)' or *'They're there to protect the police' (Glengormley)* were not uncommon.

Many of the participants perceived that complaining about police behaviour and treatment would be a 'waste of time' unless the complaint was about something serious,

Young person 1 'I reckon at the end of the day she probably gets loads and loads (of complaints) and she (Police Ombudsman) probably wouldn't take yours into account unless it was really serious'.

Young person 2 'If it wasn't serious you wouldn't bother.'

Others felt that complaining, no matter what the nature of the incident, would not be worthwhile,

'they would never go against the police, the courts will always believe the police anyway' (Belfast).

One young male who had put a complaint through to the Office via his solicitor felt that it had been worthwhile,

'Well it all adds up I mean if one person complains and another person complains soon it will be hundreds and you have to let them know what is actually happening' (Belfast).

However another young male felt that his experience was very different,

'It was like complaining to a wall because nothing was going to be done about it anyway ... the police will just deny it or say there was no evidence to prove it' (Belfast).

Two members of one group in a loyalist area of Belfast had made complaints to the Police Ombudsman's Office but both said bluntly *'Fuck all happened'*. When the facilitator probed the boys about the issue it became clear that something had happened but the outcome was not what they had desired, *'we only got a letter ... but me ma opened it'*.

The involvement of parents in the complaints process was common with some young people not fully aware of the process or the outcome. Another individual felt his complaint was *'a waste of time'* as he only had one brief meeting, and this did not produce a favourable outcome,

'I was only at one meeting and my case was closed after that meeting it was only on for about half an hour' (Belfast).

It is difficult to comment on any of these individuals' experiences, as so often experiences are shaped by the final outcome and for many people who do not receive the outcome they desire their experiences, no matter how good, end up being negative. This was the case for the respondent, who complained about the length of his meeting,

Researcher: 'Would you have been impressed (with the Police Ombudsman's Office) if the outcome had been different?

Yes, if they still had my case going and if there had been something carried out, like a charge against the police, instead of just saying 'aye right you got hit that was it' and close the case' (Belfast).

Some individuals also said that they were hesitant of complaining due to fear of reprisals,

'if you make a complaint against the police ... they are going to watch you even more' (Belfast).

'They would aggravate you and watch you even more if you did complain' (Dungannon).

Some young people even commented that they would not feel safe handing over information *'you wouldn't know who would get hold of it'*. This suggests that some young people do not see the Police Ombudsman as being an independent body. A NISRA survey (February 2002) found that 18% of 16-24 year olds viewed the Police Ombudsman as part of the police, while 71% considered it to be independent. The survey within this research indicated that only 28% agreed that the Police Ombudsman was independent with over half of respondents opting for the neutral response (see Table 19).

For those who had no direct experience of the Office there was a sense of the unknown and confusion at how the complaint would be dealt with. Questions were asked such as *'would they listen and how would they investigate?'* and *'would our complaint be investigated properly?'*. This led the young people to recommend that the Office should be more widely publicised and suggestions were made as to how knowledge could be increased.

5.4 Complaining

Experiences of the PSNI had led some individuals to make complaints whilst others, with similar experiences had either decided not to complain or did not know how to complain,

'I didn't make a complaint, to be truthful I didn't really know what way to go about it' *(Glengormley)*.

The reasons for and against complaining were discussed within the groups and various opinions were put forward. This section will discuss the issue of complaining against the PSNI and the complainants' views on the procedure.

Ramifications of making complaints

There was a prevalent culture demonstrated by the majority of focus group participants that it is preferable not to draw attention to oneself. The act of making a complaint against the police through whatever channels was generally expected to have either no result at all or a negative result, *'You'd only get stopped more often'*. Concern that whether a complaint was upheld or not by the Police Ombudsman, the very act of registering a complaint would mean that the police would *'aggravate you and watch you even more if you did'*.

Reasons for complaining

'I'd only complain if they hit me' *(Monkstown)*.

Most of the young people felt that the action that merited a complaint had to be serious otherwise it would be ignored and viewed as trivial. When this issue was pursued it was generally felt that 'serious' meant physical assault, while complaints about other forms of police behaviour such as verbal abuse and harassment would not be taken seriously,

'I reckon at the end of the day she probably gets loads and loads (of complaints) and she (Police Ombudsman) probably wouldn't take yours into account unless it was really serious.

Researcher: What would you view as serious?

If you seen some kind of injustice you know if you saw something like somebody being beat up'

However, there were other issues which were important to young people including lesser forms of harassment such as verbal abuse, being moved along, sitting outside their houses or at meeting places and being watched, that the young people felt they could not complain about,

'You would feel stupid complaining for such a small thing' (on police attitude and ways of talking to young people) (Fermanagh).

'You would be laughed to because you're a kid' (Belfast).

In theory many felt that if an individual felt unfairly treated this was enough to justify a complaint but in reality this probably would not be the case,

'I think in theory if you believe that you have been treated unfairly that would be a reason for you to go to the Ombudsman but I think in reality people would feel that they would need to be physically attacked or verbally abused – strongly verbally abused before they would consider approaching the Ombudsman' (Glengormley).

Reasons for not complaining

The quantitative study asked 'if you had problems with the police but chose not to complain why did you not do so?'. Table 20 documents the results of the respondents who chose not to complain (382 respondents, 33% of the total).

Table 20 Reasons for not complaining

Reason	Frequency	Percentage
Police would not do anything	226	59
Incident was not serious enough	48	13
Could not be bothered	40	10
Did not know how to complain	24	6
Scared of police reprisals	34	9
Other	10	3
Total	382	100

Within the focus groups there was a perception that the issues considered to be important to young people would be seen as less significant by the Police Ombudsman. Therefore, their importance would be minimised by the systems set in place by the more powerful Ombudsman, *'they would be too busy to deal with 'lesser complaints.' (Glengormley)*.

From one Belfast group there was an overriding feeling that,

'small things would be laughed at or ignored, for example being followed around in shops' (Belfast).

1. **Lack of Knowledge**: For some who did not complain the simple reason was that they did not know how to,

'I would have complained to her, but I didn't know how to' (Glengormley).

This led some of the young people to request more information about how and who to complain to and the complaints procedure itself. One group commented on the *South City Beat* television programme about the PSNI in South Belfast and thought a similar programme could follow complaints,

'I thought that (South City Beat) was a really good series ... Maybe the Ombudsman could produce something ... a case where Joe Bloggs takes a complaint ... I have never heard the Ombudsman publicising' (Glengormley).

2. **Accessibility**: For some there was also an issue of accessibility as there was no local Office in their area for them to call in and lodge a complaint,

'If there was an Office in Derry I would go in and see about it (complaint)'.

'Their Office isn't massively accessible' (Derry Londonderry).

As noted above one young woman who worked in the Citizen's Advice Bureau told her group that the Police Ombudsman's Office *'use our offices for interviews'*, but none of the other group members were aware that this was the case. This again highlights the lack of knowledge of the operations of the Police Ombudsman's Office and of the ways that people can complain about police behaviour.

3. **Support for the Police**: There were a number of respondents who were reluctant to complain due to their overall support of the police,

'You don't want to go against them if you are sympathetic to the difficulties of policing'.

4. **Pointless**: Among those who had decided not to complain there was an overwhelming feeling that there was 'no point',

'... there's no point in putting a complaint in ... nothing happens' (Larne).

It was felt that their version of events would not be believed,

'... the courts will always believe the police anyway' and *'it's my word against the police officers'* (Belfast).

One group indicated that complaining through the Police Ombudsman would be useless as *'they are bound to show favouritism to the police'.* This belief in 'favouritism' towards the police led to discussions on the impartial nature of the Police Ombudsman. As noted above many young people felt that the organisation was just another division of the police and not a separate or independent organisation. The inclusion of 'police' in the name underpinned this sense of connection for some,

'The name Police Ombudsman makes people think they are something to do with the police' (Belfast).

5. **Too Much Hassle**: Other young people simply said that they felt that it was not worth the hassle to make a complaint and it was easier to accept the situation and get on with life,

'to be honest with you I couldn't be bothered with the hassle' (Ballymena).

The perceived hassle of making a complaint indicated that some do not view the procedure to be 'user friendly'. In addition some young people feared that they would be subjected to further harassment or reprisals if they complained,

'... if you make a complaint against the police ... they are going to watch you even more' (Belfast).

6. **Nothing To Gain**: One young female said that she didn't complain because she had nothing to gain. She had witnessed a man being beaten but didn't complain as,

'there was no likelihood of getting any compensation for herself' (Derry Londonderry).

However, this attitude was not echoed by the rest of the group, who felt that 'the police shouldn't cross the line' and that only by complaining could police boundaries be established.

The procedure of complaining

For many participants the formal procedure of complaining was considered to be daunting (the procedure is set out in Appendix 2). For some people the lack of knowledge only served to increase their fear about the procedure. Within the focus groups only a few participants had actually made a formal complaint but many others said that they would have liked to but did not know how or just hadn't bothered.

Those who had complained made their complaints at a variety of locations. Some had lodged the complaint at a police station, although some had said they had been reluctant to complain in this way because of fear of reprisals. Others had made a complaint direct to the Police Ombudsman's Office, at a Citizen's Advice Bureau or through their MLA. Table 17 shows the organisations/individuals that complainants approached to voice their complaint

For those who had complained to the Police Ombudsman the complaint had been mainly made through a solicitor. Some of the young people said that their parents had taken charge of the complaint and they themselves had little to do with the actual procedure,

'I didn't complain myself, but my mum and dad did, through the solicitor to the Ombudsman' (Belfast).

However the majority of young people who felt that they had cause for complaint against the police chose not to initiate a formal process as they felt that the issue was too trivial. This caused frustration and some young people suggested that they needed somewhere to lodge dissatisfaction with the police service as well as complaints. One young person suggested that the Police Ombudsman's Office should have separate departments for different types of complaint, a complaints section for more serious situations that required investigation and a separate department to lodge general dissatisfaction.

The Outcome

Some of the young people who had lodged a complaint were not happy with the outcome. The survey revealed that 15 of the 24 respondents (62%) who had contacted the Police Ombudsman's Office were not happy with the service they had received. Table 21 highlights the reasons for their dissatisfaction. One young male in the focus groups felt that there had been no point complaining as nothing was done, *'... there's no point ... there's nothing done'*. However, another individual felt that even though the outcome was not what he had desired it was still worth complaining as the complaints might add up and then someone would have to listen.

Table 21 Reason for not being happy with the service from the Police Ombudsman

Reason	Frequency	Percentage
Slow Response	5	33
Did not take complaint seriously	5	33
Did not hear anything after making complaint	2	13
Did not follow up complaint	2	13
Process took a long time	1	6
Total	15	100

One participant who had been unhappy with the Police Ombudsman's handling of his complaint admitted that his dissatisfaction arose from not receiving the outcome he had desired,

'Fuck all happened ... I just got a letter and nothing was done' (Belfast).

For many the final outcome of any complaint would be to see the police officer against which the complaint was made be disciplined to ensure that no one else would suffer,

'I would like to see discipline ... something really done about it like ... for people in the future' *(Belfast).*

One young man said that all he wanted was 'guarantees that action would be taken' and to be kept informed whilst the investigation was being carried out.

'While they carry out the investigation it would be good if they kept in touch' *(Belfast).*

The lack of any information about the nature of the investigation made this participant feel that things were being concealed.

A few of the participants said that their motive for complaining would be financial and they would want compensation, *'All I want is compensation, to make something out of it'* *(Hydebank).* But others within this group disagreed and said that an apology and a change in the way they were treated were more important. For the young people who took part in this research there was a desire to have their complaints and sense of dissatisfaction towards the police recognised and for them to be listened to. This was something that many of the young people felt never happened and this left them feeling worthless and unimportant.

6. The Policing Board and District Policing Partnerships

6.1 Quantitative findings

The survey found that 65% of respondents had heard of the Policing Board. This is substantially lower than the Northern Ireland Omnibus survey (2002), which found 80% of under 25s had heard of the Board. However, it has to be highlighted that the Northern Ireland Omnibus only surveyed 127 under 25s compared to this study with a sample of 1163. Awareness was higher among the older participants (69% of 22-24 year olds being aware compared to only 54% of under 16s) and also among those with the higher educational attainments: A-levels (63%), NVQs (72%) and HND/Degree (73%) compared with 39% with no formal qualifications (39%). However, there was little difference between Catholics and Protestants (66% and 65%).

There was less certainty of the role of the Policing Board. Of the 65% who claimed to be aware of its role, 45% saw the role of the Board 'to oversee policing and hold the Chief Constable and the PSNI to account'. This compares to 66% of under 25s who identified this role in the Northern Ireland Omnibus survey. However, only around 27% were aware of its responsibility to set policing priorities and targets (Table 22).

Table 22 What do you think the role of the Policing Board is?

Role	ICRSurvey (2003) Percentage	NI Omnibus survey (2002) Percentage
To oversee policing and hold the Chief Constable and the PSNI to account	45	66
Set policing priorities	27	
Set policing targets	27	
Don't Know	23	6
To tell the police what to do	11	24
To tell the Chief Constable what to do	5	3

(participants were allowed to tick more than one)

In terms of the Board's impartiality 60% indicated a neutral response of neither agree nor disagree with 22% either agreeing (21%) or strongly agreeing (1%) and 18% either disagreeing (13%) or strongly disagreeing (5%). Disagreement was higher among the Catholic community with

26% either disagreeing or strongly disagreeing compared to 10% of the Protestant community (Figure 2).

The Board's independence from the police was also investigated with the largest percentage (51%) opting for the neutral response. Only 23% agreed it was independent with slightly less disagreeing (20%). This figure of 23% is substantially lower than other survey results with the Northern Ireland Omnibus Survey (2002) finding that 57% of under 25s viewed the Board as independent from the police.

Figure 2 The Board's impartiality according to community background

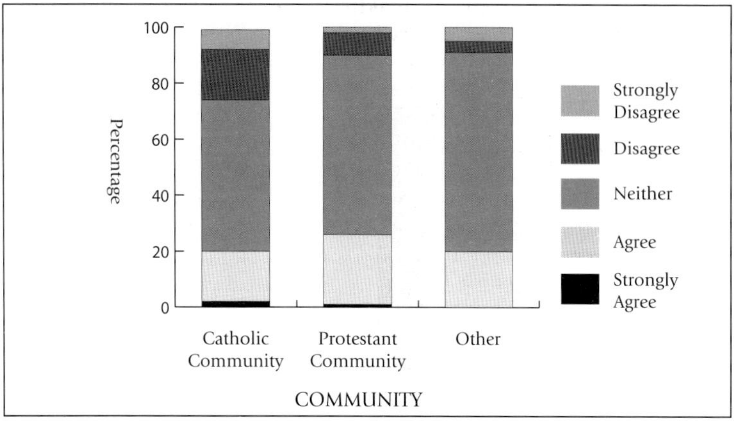

Figure 3 The Board's independence according to community background

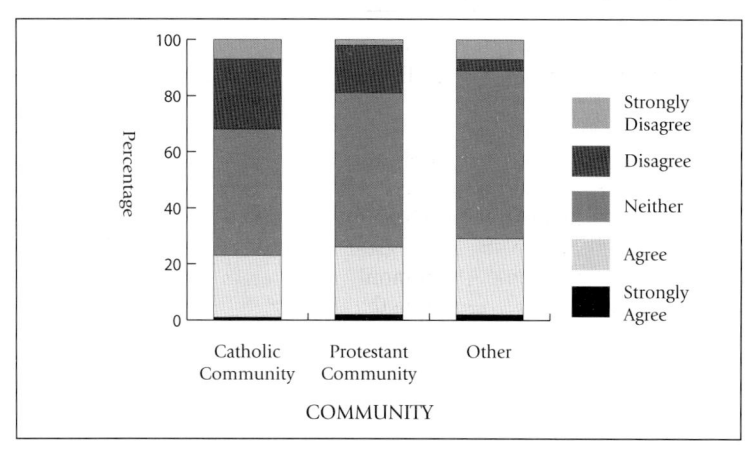

The Catholic community (32% disagreeing or strongly disagreeing) were less inclined than the Protestant community (18% disagreeing or strongly disagreeing) to view the Board as independent as Figure 3 illustrates.

Only 20% agreed that the Board had made policing more effective and efficient, however, 59% neither agreed nor disagreed and 14% disagreed. Again the disagreement was higher among the Catholic community with 24% disagreeing or strongly disagreeing compared to 16% of the Protestant community (Figure 4).

Figure 4 The Board's role in making policing more effective and efficient according to community background

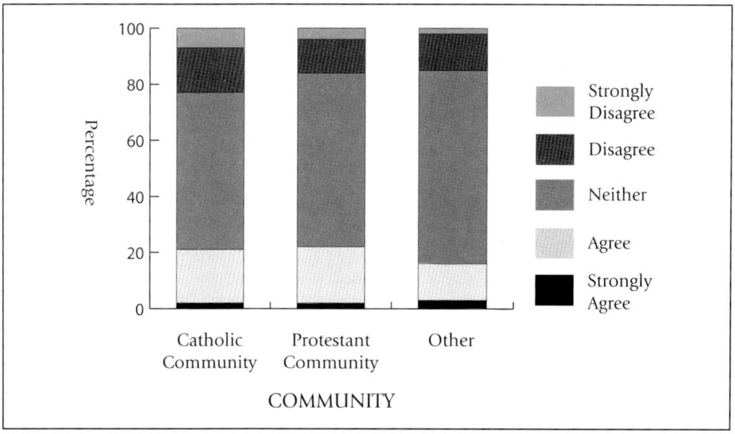

Less than one quarter of respondents (24%) had heard of DPPs with 18% of these admitting that they did not know what their role was (Table 23).

Awareness was greater among those within the higher educational bracket (30% compared to 17% of those with no formal qualification). This lack of knowledge of the DPPs and indeed the Policing Board meant that discussions within the focus groups were limited in conjunction with these organisations. A commonly asked question was 'what are they?' with young people admitting that their knowledge was limited.

Table 23 What do you think the role of the DPPs is?

Role	Frequency	Percentage
Haven't heard of the DPPs	880	77
Don't know what their role is	204	18
To oversee policing at a local level	168	15
Set policing priorities	98	8
Set local policing targets	91	8
To tell the police what to do	21	2
To tell the District Commander what to do	21	2

(participants were allowed to tick more than one)

6.2 Attitudes and Knowledge of Policing Board

As the quantitative findings suggest information about the Policing Board and knowledge of any potential DPPs was scant. Although many knew of, or had heard of, the Policing Board they had little understanding of the role of the organisation. For some there was confusion with other organisations,

'are they the ones that take on if you can march or not?' (Derry Londonderry).

One issue that had registered in relation to the Policing Board was in relation to the membership. Concern was raised in some groups about the involvement of those with criminal records or custodial sentences or members of political parties. A group in Fermanagh felt that this may lead to the politicisation of the police service,

'the police service is a big thing, they run your community and country so maybe not political prisoners, but maybe other small time criminals.'

In contrast participants in the focus group at Hydebank Young Offenders Centre felt that those with custodial sentences should be allowed to join police boards. There was also concern that young people's interests and experiences were not represented on the Board.

6.3 Attitudes and Knowledge of DPPs

Generally participants were unfamiliar with the DPPs that were currently being established. The most concise understanding came from a group in Craigavon,

'it's local policing throughout the areas working at a community level' (Craigavon).

While participants felt that young people should have an opportunity to express their views, most were reluctant to get involved in any way with the DPPs. For some this reluctance was due to the 'cool factor', getting involved in a policing forum would leave you open to teasing from your mates,

'it's just not worth the hassle you'd get from your mates' (Glengormley).

'it's not worth the hassle' (Ballymena).

Some cited a fear of more serious responses from sections within their own communities, while for others it was clear that there was a lack of trust about the reasons for the DPPs with some people making sinister suggestions that the new boards were simply another means of intelligence gathering and that *'you'd just be a tout - it's a sad excuse for getting more touts (Belfast)'*. Some people expressed a fear that getting involved could lead to *'reprisals from the community'*.

Young people who identified themselves as 'hoods' also voiced reservations about the structuring of the DPPs. They voiced a concern that as they were likely to be represented from within communities dominated by paramilitary voices, they would be further peripheralised due to their lack of support for and by those paramilitaries.

This attitude of the involvement of those with criminal records/custodial sentences was also of concern to participants who were non-offenders or not perceived to be at risk of offending. Many displayed mixed attitudes suggesting that while ex-offenders would have a degree of insight into the community they were concerned that only those 'powerful' within the community (ex-political prisoners) would be in a position to involve themselves, *'They should voice their opinion but have no authority' (Belfast).*

One Belfast group's response was that participation in the DPPs would not benefit the young but rather would simply reinforce the status of certain community leaders, *'it's all right for them 'uns, they sit in their wee offices and get paid for it while we get lifted. We get beat and they get the money' (Belfast).*

Young people within these communities felt that the DPPs would have to have some clear benefit for them before they would be prepared to participate or engage in any way. As with other areas of policing, it appeared that there was an inbuilt understanding that to be involved in policing was a 'political' act and therefore those who would become involved would have their own political rather than civil motives. Interestingly these suspicions and the reluctance to engage with, or participate in, the new accountability structures were expressed equally by both Protestant and Catholic young people.

As the opportunity for representation on the DPPs is predicated by community representation in geographical terms, a number of participants commented on how this criteria rules out an effective participation of those ethnic minority groups whose sense of community is not determined by one particular area of residency.

6.4 Experiences of the Policing Board and DPPs

Few of the young people had any experiences with the Policing Board but some expressed an interest in obtaining more information. More people had an awareness of the move to promote DPPs especially those living in highly politicised Protestant areas. However, this was not found in the quantitative study with both communities having similar levels of awareness.

7. Suggestions

The following suggestions are based on ideas generated within the discussion groups with the young people.

7.1 General Suggestions

Need for Transparency
The general suggestion made was the need for more transparency from all of the organisations. Throughout the discussion groups, participants suggested how the issues of engagement and transparency could be tackled within policing organisations and these were used within other groups as basis for discussion. Many suggestions were eagerly picked up and encouraged debate within the groups.

Outreach
It was also suggested that the both the police and the Police Ombudsman's Office should engage in more outreach work to increase knowledge and understanding. It was further recommended that this should be conducted at an inter-generational level beginning with pre-schoolers to encourage debate and support from within the family and educational systems.

7.2 Police

One group commented that young people's attitudes towards the police were *'so poor, anything done would need to be radical'* (Ballymena).

Informal engagement
Generally practices within the police service were seen to dehumanise civilians' perceptions of officers and many young people suggested that an informal engagement with the police would be welcome. One Catholic woman from Belfast suggested there should be a committee within the police service made up of wives and family members who could send out a newsletter with their personal stories/experiences so that people could hear the human side rather than the professional side of the police and so *'they could be seen as people who have suffered as well as making other's suffer'*.

Building confidence in DPP/PB/PSNI
The following are suggestions from the young people as to how confidence of policing and policing organisations could be built among young people. The suggestions range from adapting behaviour to increasing outreach:

Behaviour
- More approachable, *'even if they would say hello when they see you'*;
- More helpful, *'if they could even pretend they were trying to make more effort over little things that matter to us'*;
- More understanding, *'if they were to take people's worries more seriously it would show they respect everyone'*;
- More accessible and easier to contact;
- Stop pre-judging young people;
- Become less physically threatening, *'Leave their batons in their pockets'*.

Communication
- Take an interest in things young people are interested in for example work on community radio programmes;
- Learn to listen and engage with young people, not ask too many questions but listen to what they say;
- Literature should be more youth friendly.

Outreach
- More outreach, *'They should have a specially active department just for dealing with outreach for young people'*;
- More community involved activities, 'they *should do more social things like 'community fun days' and football competitions'*;
- More pre-school engagement, *'They should start working with young children so that parent's views do not contaminate children'*;
- Organising more training opportunities for young people – police cadets;
- Advertise for people to come in for work experience.

7.3 Police Ombudsman's Office

Feedback
Participants who had made a formal complaint against the police indicated that they would like to have more feedback and updating on the progress of their complaint.

Increase Awareness
Some groups suggested that the Office should have a public awareness campaign to increase consumer awareness of its role and procedures. In spite of the Office producing information leaflets and providing talks none of the respondents had received any information.Group discussions perceived that the most far reaching effects would come by advertising on TV in a documentary style that would personalise the narrative elements within the work and be followed up with key images in, for example, newspapers, on the back of buses and in college libraries.

This would be supplemented by the personal narratives of the police, their families and the complainants to personalise the situations, *'At the end of the day they're all human beings' (Craigavon)* and *'True life stories always get to you' (Derry Londonderry)*. The young people drew on the South City Beat model – *'it was class, it was about our nightclubs and things' (Belfast)*.

It was also felt that more general information about how to contact the Office should be publicised by;
- Youth-friendly posters in venues used by young people such as the dole office, church, youth centres, nightclubs, school and colleges. This idea was based on a poster by the Children's Law Centre on age and rights;
- Newspapers;
- Back of buses;
- Child benefit books;
- Road shows that told the stories not just the process;
- Having a freephone number.

Outcome of complaints
Some individuals within groups emphasised the incentive of compensation whilst others were more satisfied with a personalised and full apology with explanations and acknowledgments of their actions. However, whatever the outcome the young people wanted to be informed and feel that their complaint had been fairly dealt with.

Structure
It was also suggested that there should be a separate department within the Office dedicated to young people, for dealing with small complaints (like being followed in the town/round shops). This would enable complaints to be registered, even when there was a minimum/lack of evidence on the part of the complainant.

It was also felt that the Police Ombudsman's Office would be seen to raise its profile and demonstrate its impartiality if it were to take a more active role in lobbying for more transparent policing policies such as cameras inside police land rovers to record what happens and as one interviewee commented, *'we never have evidence, if they want it they should put cameras inside police Land Rovers to see what they do' (Hydebank)*.

8. Recommendations

The following recommendations are based on the research findings documented in this report:

Police Ombudsman for Northern Ireland

1. There is still clearly a need to promote greater awareness of the organisation and its work among young people. This appears to be particularly important for young people living outside of Belfast. One option would be to organise a more focused and intensive road show or out-reach programme involving presentations in schools and youth organisations. Many young people have some knowledge of the Police Ombudsman's Office but that knowledge is lacking in depth and an outreach programme should aim to build upon existing knowledge, rather than focus on providing very basic information.

2. Information for young people on the Office should be more attractive and appropriate to a young audience. Designing this material will require some consultation and discussion with young people. It might therefore be appropriate to convene an advisory group of young people for say a six month period to discuss in more detail how the Police Ombudsman's Office might make their information and services more accessible to young people.

3. A number of young people commented on the *South City Beat* programme and suggested a similar programme on the Office would be of interest. The Police Ombudsman's Office could approach one of the local TV companies and suggest the idea of a documentary on the work of the organisation. Such a programme might be made more relevant by exploring the complaints process from a young person's perspective.

4. There is also a need to increase awareness of practical matters such as where people can go to lodge complaints other than the Police Ombudsman's Office, the police or through a solicitor. No young person had lodged a complaint through a Citizen's Advice Bureau for example. There should be a wider range of outlets throughout Northern Ireland for people to go to lodge complaints and a promotion of those which already exist. One option would be to have a Police Ombudsman logo that could be used to advertise where to lodge a complaint.

5. Many young people commented how the Office was Belfast based. It would therefore be worth exploring options for the Police Ombudsman's Office to have Offices in other areas to promote a presence outside Belfast. These could be organised as surgery style offices whereby a representative of the Police Ombudsman's Office would attend different towns on a monthly basis.

6. Preliminary complaints can be made to a range of third parties (including solicitors, politicians, CABs) who forward these to the Police Ombudsman's Office. At present these initial complaints include a variable quality of information about the complainant. We believe it would be useful to develop a simple standardised complaint registration form, or to ensure widespread availability of the current form, for all those agencies and organisations that forward complaints against police officers. This will assist the Police Ombudsman's research branch in their data collection and analysis.

7. Finally given the large number of complaints made by young people it would be worth considering creating a team within Police Ombudsman's Office who specifically deal with complaints by young people and produce information especially for them. This would enable specialist knowledge to be developed and information to be gained on problems experienced by young people and best methods of responding to them.

Policing Board

8. There is clearly a need to promote greater awareness of the Policing Board, the DPPs and their role in creating police accountability in Northern Ireland. The Policing Board should consider options for an outreach programme to engage with young people through schools and youth organisations.

9. The programme should aim to provide a range of information to young people on all aspects of policing. This information would need to be youth friendly and would need to be designed in consultation with young people.

10. The research raised a number of issues where young people felt they were treated badly by the police, however young people's views are rarely taken into account in any formal way, there are no young people on the Policing Board and the latest policing plan fails to mention young people in any of its aims or targets. It would be appropriate for

the Board to initiate some form of ongoing consultation with young people on policing issues. This could be done by either creating a consultative body of young people, or having an ongoing programme of devolved consultations or through regular surveys of young people's attitudes.

11. The Board should raise the issues in this report with the Chief Constable and work together to ensure the PSNI develops a programme that encourages more effective engagement between the police and young people. Many young people clearly have regard for the police and expressed a desire for more constructive interactions.

12. The Board should also discuss how the current training programmes within the PSNI deal with the policing of young people. Many young people felt that police officers had little sympathy for them or a lack of understanding of their situation. The Policing Board should task the PSNI to consider how these issues could be addressed within both recruitment training and any training delivered through DCUs.

References

Anderson, S., Kinsey, R., Loader, I. and Smith, C. (1994) *Cautionary Tales: Young People, Crime and Policing in Edinburgh*. Aldershot, Avebury.

Bell. J. (1993) *Doing your research project: a guide for first time researchers in education and social science*. Milton Keynes, Open University Press.

Bowling, B. and Phillips, C. (2002) *Racism, Crime and Justice*. Harlow, Longman.

Brewer, J. and Magee, K. (1991) *Inside the RUC*. Oxford, Clarendon Press.

Brown, D. (1987) *The Police Complaints Procedure: A Survey of Complainants Views*. Home Office Research Study 93. London, HMSO.

Cashmore, E. and McLaughlin, E. (eds) (1991) *Out of Order: Policing Black People*. London, Routledge.

Connolly, P., Smith, A. and Kelly, B. (2002) *Too Young to Notice? The Cultural and Political Awareness of 3-6 year olds in Northern Ireland*. Belfast, CRC.

Cotton, J. and Povey, D. (1999) *Police Complaints and Discipline: England and Wales, April 1998 to March 1999*. London, Home Office.

Cotton, J. and Povey, D. (2000) *Police Complaints and Discipline: England and Wales, April 1999 to March 2000*. London, Home Office.

Donnelly, D. and Scott, K. (2002) Police Accountability in Scotland: (2) 'New' Accountability. *The Police Journal* Vol 75:1 56-66.

Ellison, G. (2001) *Young People, Crime, Policing and Victimisation in Northern Ireland*. Belfast, Institute of Criminology, Queen's University Belfast.

Ellison, G. and Smyth, J. (2000) *The Crowned Harp: Policing Northern Ireland*. London, Pluto Press.

Ferrel, J. (1995) Culture, Crime and Cultural Criminology. *Journal of Criminal Justice and Popular Culture* Vol 3:2 25-42.

Goldsmith, A. and Lewis, C. (2000) *Civilian Oversight of Policing: Governance, Democracy and Human Rights*. Oxford, Hart Publishing.

Hague, L. and Willis, M. (2001) *Views on the Northern Ireland Policing Board: Findings from the March 2001 Northern Ireland Omnibus Survey*. Belfast, NIO.

Hamilton, A., Moore, L. and Trimble, T. (1995) *Policing a Divided Society: Issues and Perceptions in Northern Ireland*. Coleraine, Centre for the Study of Conflict.

Hartless, J., Ditton, J., Nair, G. and Philips, S. (1995) More Sinned Against Than Sinning: A Study of Teenagers Experience of Crime. *British Journal of Criminology* Vol 35:1 114-133.

Hayes, M. (1997) *A Police Ombudsman for Northern Ireland? A Review of the Police Complaints System in Northern Ireland*. Belfast, Stationary Office.

HMIC for Scotland (2000) *A Fair Cop: The Investigation of Complaints Against the Police in Scotland*. Edinburgh, Stationary Office.

Jarman, N. and O'Halloran, C. (2001) Recreational Rioting: Young People, Interface Areas and Violence. *Child Care in Practice* Vol 7:1 2-16.

Jarman, N., Quinn, G, Murphy, J. and Nichol, S. (2002) Escaping to the Happy Planet? Drug Use, Education and Professional Support in North Belfast. *Child Care in Practice* Vol 8:3 159-175.

Kennison, P. (2002) Policing Diversity – Managing Complaints Against the Police. *The Police Journal* Vol 75:117-135.

Lee. M. (1998) *Youth Crime and Police Work*. Basingstoke, Macmillan.

Lewis, C. (1999) *Complaints Against the Police: The Politics of Reform*. Sydney, Hawkins Press.

Loader, I. (1996) *Youth, Policing and Democracy*. Basingstoke, Macmillan.

McGarry, J. and O'Leary, B. (1999) *Policing Northern Ireland: Proposals for a New Start*. Belfast, Blackstaff Press.

McLaughlin, E. (1991) Police Accountability and Black People: Into the 1990s. In Cashmore, E. and McLaughlin, E. (eds) *Out of Order: Policing Black People*. London, Routledge.

McLaughlin, E. and Johansen, A. (2002) A Force for Change? The Prospects of Applying Restorative Justice to Citizen Complaints against the Police in England and Wales. *British Journal of Criminology* 42:635-653.

McVeigh, R. (1994) *'It's Part of Life Here': The Security Forces and Harassment in Northern Ireland*. Belfast, CAJ.

Maguire, M. and Corbett, C. (1991) *A Study of the Police Complaints System*. London, HMSO.

Maguire, M. and Wilson, D. (2002) *Views on the Northern Ireland Policing Board: Findings from the October 2001 Northern Ireland Omnibus Survey*. Belfast, NIO.

Muncie, J. (1999) *Youth Crime: A Critical Introduction*. London, Sage.

Newburn, T. and Stanko, E. (1994) *Just Boys Doing Business? Men, Masculinities and Crime*. London, Routledge.

NIO Statistics and Research Branch (2003) *A Commentary of Northern Ireland Crime Statistics 2001*. Belfast, NIO.

O'Mahony, D., Geary, R., McEvoy, K. and Morison, J. (2000) *Crime, Community and Locale: The Northern Ireland Communities Crime Survey*. Aldershot, Ashgate.

O'Rawe, M. and Moore, L. (1997) *Human Rights on Duty: Principles for Better Policing – International Lessons for Northern Ireland.* Belfast, CAJ.

O'Rawe, M. and Moore, L. (2000) Accountability and Police Complaints in Northern Ireland: Leaving the Past Behind? In Goldsmith, A. and Lewis, C. (eds). *Civilian Oversight of Policing: Governance, Democracy and Human Rights.* Oxford, Hart Publishing.

Palmiotto, M. (ed) (2001) Police Misconduct: A Reader for the 21st Century. New Jersey, Prentice Hall.

Police Ombudsman for Northern Ireland (2001a) *Public Awareness of the Northern Ireland Police Complaints System: Research Report Number 1.* Belfast, Police Ombudsman's Office

Police Ombudsman for Northern Ireland (2001b) *Public Awareness of the Northern Ireland Police Complaints System: Research Report Number 2.* Belfast, Police Ombudsman's Office

Police Ombudsman for Northern Ireland (2002) *Public Awareness of the Northern Ireland Police Complaints System 2002: Research Report 2/2002.* Belfast, Police Ombudsman's Office.

Royal Ulster Constabulary (2001) *Report of the Chief Constable.* Knock, RUC.

Russell, K. (1976) *Complaints Against the Police: A Sociological View.* Leicester, Milltak.

Ryder, C. (2000) *The RUC 1922-2000: A Force Under Fire.* London, Arrow Books.

Scarman, L (1981) *The Brixton Disorders 10-12 April 1981: Report of an Inquiry.* London, Stationary Office.

Smyth, M., Hamilton, J. and Thomson, K. (2001) *Creggan Community Restorative Justice: An evaluation and suggested way forward.* Belfast, ICR.

Stol, W. and Bervoets, E. (2002) Policing Dutch-Moroccan Youth. *Policing and Society* Vol 12:3 191-200.

Thomassen, G. (2002) Investigating Complaints Against the Police in Norway: An Empirical Evaluation. *Policing and Society* Vol 12:3 201-210.

Waddington, P. (1999) *Policing Citizens: Authority and Rights.* London, UCL Press.

Walker, S. (1999) Citizen Complaints and the Community. In Kenney, D. and McNamara, R. (eds) *Police and Policing: Contemporary Issues.* Westport CT, Praeger.

Weitzer, R. (1995) *Policing Under Fire: Ethnic Relations and Police Community Relations in Northern Ireland.* New York, SUNY.

Wright, J. and Bryett, K. (2000) *Policing and Conflict in Northern Ireland.* Basingstoke, Macmillan.

Appendix 1 Questionnaire

Young People and the Police
A survey to assess the attitudes of young people towards the Police, Police Ombudsman's Office and Policing Board.
Please read the following questions carefully and answer according to your own experience.
This questionnaire has been designed by the Institute for Conflict Research (ICR) and is funded by the Police Ombudsman's Office and the Policing Board.

DEMOGRAPHICS

For official use only
Serial Number
☐ ☐ ☐ ☐

1. How old are you?
   Under 16   16-18   19-21   22-24
   ☐   ☐   ☐   ☐

2. Are you:
   ☐ Male   ☐ Female

3. What town/village do you live in?

....

4. What is your postcode?   BT.............................

5. In terms of the two communities in Northern Ireland are you considered to be (tick one)
   ☐ A member of the Catholic community
   ☐ A member of the Protestant community

Other (please state)...

6. In terms of your ethnic background are you (tick one)
   - ☐ White   ☐ Chinese   ☐ Irish Traveller
   - ☐ Indian   ☐ Pakistani ☐ Bangladeshi
   - ☐ Black Caribbean   ☐ Black African
   - ☐ Black Other   ☐ Mixed ethnic group (please state)

   ....
   - ☐ Other (please state)

....
7. Are you currently (tick one)
   - ☐ At school   ☐ At college   ☐ University   ☐ Working
   - ☐ In full time training   ☐ Unemployed
   - ☐ Other (please state)...

8. What is the highest level of educational qualification you have obtained or are currently studying for? (tick one)
   - ☐ None   ☐ GCSEs   ☐ A-Levels or equivalent
   - ☐ NVQ/BTEC   ☐ HND/Degree or higher
   - ☐ Other (please state)..

ATTITUDES TOWARDS THE POLICE

9. Have you been in contact with the PSNI in the past 12 months?
   - ☐ Yes   ☐ No

10. If yes, what form did this contact take? If more than once state most recent contact.
   - ☐ You haven't had any contact (go to question 13)
   - ☐ You were a victim of crime
   - ☐ You witnessed a crime
   - ☐ Required to produce driving documents
   - ☐ You were a perpetrator of crime
   - ☐ You were stopped and questioned
   - ☐ You were asked to move on

☐ Other (please state)..

11. Was this contact…
    ☐ On the street   ☐ At home
    ☐ At school/college/work ☐ At a public house
    ☐ At a club
    ☐ Other (please state)..

12. How satisfied were you with the PSNI during this contact?
    ☐ Very satisfied   ☐ Satisfied
    ☐ Neither satisfied nor dissatisfied   ☐ Dissatisfied
    ☐ Very dissatisfied

13. Has a police officer ever behaved in an unacceptable way towards you in the past 12 months?
    ☐ Yes   ☐ No (go to question 16)

14. How many times has this happened in the past 12 months?

....

15. List types of unacceptable behaviour you have experienced in the past 12 months? (tick all that apply)
    ☐ Disrespectful or impolite
    ☐ Harassment
    ☐ Did not follow proper procedures
    ☐ Stopped or searched without reason
    ☐ Discrimination due to race, gender
    ☐ Wrongly accused of misbehaviour
    ☐ Used sectarian, racist or sexist language
    ☐ Behaved in violent way
    ☐ Swore
    ☐ Did not carry out duty properly

☐ Searched house without reason
☐ Took an item of property
☐ Other (please state) ....

Indicate how much you agree or disagree with the following statements

16. Overall, I believe the police to be honest
    ☐ Strongly agree
    ☐ Agree
    ☐ Neither agree nor disagree
    ☐ Disagree
    ☐ Strongly disagree

17. Overall, I believe the police to be professional
    ☐ Strongly agree
    ☐ Agree
    ☐ Neither agree nor disagree
    ☐ Disagree
    ☐ Strongly disagree

18. Overall, I believe the police to be helpful
    ☐ Strongly agree
    ☐ Agree
    ☐ Neither agree nor disagree
    ☐ Disagree
    ☐ Strongly disagree

19. Overall, I believe the police to be fair
    ☐ Strongly agree
    ☐ Agree
    ☐ Neither agree nor disagree
    ☐ Disagree
    ☐ Strongly disagree

20. Overall, I believe the police to be there for my protection
    ☐ Strongly agree
    ☐ Agree
    ☐ Neither agree nor disagree
    ☐ Disagree
    ☐ Strongly disagree

21. Overall, I believe the police to be able to understand youth issues
    ☐ Strongly agree
    ☐ Agree
    ☐ Neither agree nor disagree
    ☐ Disagree
    ☐ Strongly disagree

22. Overall, I believe the police to be able to solve community problems
    ☐ Strongly agree
    ☐ Agree
    ☐ Neither agree nor disagree
    ☐ Disagree
    ☐ Strongly disagree

23. Overall, I believe the police to be acceptable
    ☐ Strongly agree
    ☐ Agree
    ☐ Neither agree nor disagree
    ☐ Disagree
    ☐ Strongly disagree

24. Overall, I believe the police to be from my community
    ☐ Strongly agree
    ☐ Agree
    ☐ Neither agree nor disagree
    ☐ Disagree
    ☐ Strongly disagree

25. Overall, I believe that policing has improved since becoming the PSNI
- ☐ Strongly agree
- ☐ Agree
- ☐ Neither agree nor disagree
- ☐ Disagree
- ☐ Strongly disagree

26. Please tick the 3 main activities that in your opinion the PSNI should be concentrating on? (tick three)

☐ Assaults	☐ Car Crime
☐ Community safety	☐ Crime Prevention
☐ Domestic Burglary	☐ Drug dealing
☐ Drug Use	☐ Paramilitary Activity
☐ Prompt response to emergencies	☐ Public Disorder
☐ Road Safety	

☐ Other (please state)..

COMPLAINTS ABOUT THE POLICE

27. Have you ever made a complaint about the police in the past 12 months?
- ☐ Yes ☐ No

28. Who did you make a complaint to? (tick all that apply)
- ☐ Haven't made a complaint (go to question 31)
- ☐ Local police station   ☐ ICPC
- ☐ Solicitor   ☐ Chief Constable
- ☐ MP/MLA/Councillor   ☐ CAB
- ☐ Police Ombudsman
- ☐ Other (please state)..
- ☐ Did not know who to complain to
- ☐ Did not know how to complain
- ☐ Don't know

Appendix 1

29. If you have made a complaint were you happy with the response you received?
☐ Yes (go to question 31)
☐ No

30. If you were unhappy with the response, why were you unhappy? (tick one)
☐ Slow response
☐ Process took a long time
☐ Did not take the complaint seriously
☐ Did not hear anything after making complaint
☐ Did not follow up complaint
☐ Withdrew complaint
☐ Other (please state)...

....

31. If you have had problems with the police but chose not to complain, why did you not do so? (tick one)
☐ Haven't had any problems
☐ Police wouldn't do anything about the complaint
☐ Incident was not serious enough
☐ Could not be bothered
☐ Scared of police reprisals
☐ Did not know how to complain
☐ Other (please state)...

....

ATTITUDES TOWARDS AND KNOWLEDGE OF THE POLICE OMBUDSMAN

32. Have you heard of the Police Ombudsman's Office?
☐ Yes   ☐ No

Appendix 1

33. How did you first hear of the Police Ombudsman's Office? (tick one)
    ☐ Haven't heard of the Police Ombudsman's Office
    (go to question 35)
    ☐ Television
    ☐ Radio
    ☐ Newspapers
    ☐ Friends/family
    ☐ Leaflet/poster
    ☐ Through work
    ☐ Through school/college/university
    ☐ Other (please state)..

....

34. What do you think the role of the Police Ombudsman is? (tick all that apply)
    ☐ To receive complaints against the police
    ☐ To investigate complaints against the police
    ☐ To investigate complaints by the police
    ☐ To protect the police from investigation
    ☐ Don't know

35. Do you know how to contact the Police Ombudsman's office?
    ☐ Yes
    ☐ No

36. Have you ever contacted the Police Ombudsman's office?
    ☐ Yes
    ☐ No (go to question 39)

37. If yes, were you happy with the service received?
    ☐ Yes (go to question 39)
    ☐ No

38. If no, what was the main reason that you were unhappy? (tick one)
   ☐ Slow response
   ☐ Process took a long time
   ☐ Did not take the complaint seriously
   ☐ Did not hear anything after making complaint
   ☐ Did not follow up complaint
   ☐ Withdrew complaint
   ☐ Other (please state)..
   ....

Indicate how much you agree or disagree with the following statements

39. The Police Ombudsman will help the police do a better job
   ☐ Strongly agree
   ☐ Agree
   ☐ Neither agree nor disagree
   ☐ Disagree
   ☐ Strongly disagree

40. The Police Ombudsman is impartial
   ☐ Strongly agree
   ☐ Agree
   ☐ Neither agree nor disagree
   ☐ Disagree
   ☐ Strongly disagree

41. The Police Ombudsman is independent of the police
   ☐ Strongly agree
   ☐ Agree
   ☐ Neither agree nor disagree
   ☐ Disagree
   ☐ Strongly disagree

42. The Police Ombudsman treats a person complaining fairly
  ☐ Strongly agree
  ☐ Agree
  ☐ Neither agree nor disagree
  ☐ Disagree
  ☐ Strongly disagree

43. The Police Ombudsman investigates complaints against the police fairly
  ☐ Strongly agree
  ☐ Agree
  ☐ Neither agree nor disagree
  ☐ Disagree
  ☐ Strongly disagree

44. The Police Ombudsman is necessary
  ☐ Strongly agree
  ☐ Agree
  ☐ Neither agree nor disagree
  ☐ Disagree
  ☐ Strongly disagree

45. The Police Ombudsman can help change the police and make it more acceptable
  ☐ Strongly agree
  ☐ Agree
  ☐ Neither agree nor disagree
  ☐ Disagree
  ☐ Strongly disagree

ATTITUDES TOWARDS AND KNOWLEDGE OF THE NORTHERN IRELAND POLICING BOARD

46. Have you heard of the Northern Ireland Policing Board?
  ☐ Yes
  ☐ No

47. What do you think the role of the Policing Board is? (tick all that apply)
- ☐ Haven't heard of the Policing Board (go to question 51)
- ☐ To tell the police what to do
- ☐ To tell the Chief Constable what to do
- ☐ To oversee policing and hold the Chief Constable and the PSNI to account
- ☐ Set policing priorities
- ☐ Set policing targets
- ☐ Don't Know
- ☐ Other (please state)...

....

48. Indicate how much you agree or disagree with the following statements
The Policing Board is impartial
- ☐ Strongly agree
- ☐ Agree
- ☐ Neither agree nor disagree
- ☐ Disagree
- ☐ Strongly disagree

49. The Policing Board is independent of the police
- ☐ Strongly agree
- ☐ Agree
- ☐ Neither agree nor disagree
- ☐ Disagree
- ☐ Strongly disagree

50. The Policing Board has made policing more effective and efficient
- ☐ Strongly agree
- ☐ Agree
- ☐ Neither agree nor disagree
- ☐ Disagree
- ☐ Strongly disagree

51. Have you heard of District Policing Partnerships (DPPs)?
    ☐ Yes
    ☐ No

52. What do you think the role of the DPPs is? (tick all that apply)
    ☐ Haven't heard of the DPPs
    ☐ To tell the police what to do
    ☐ To tell the District Commander what to do
    ☐ To oversee policing at a local level
    ☐ Set local policing priorities
    ☐ Set local policing targets
    ☐ Don't Know
    ☐ Other (please state)..
    ....

53. Would you consider joining the PSNI?
    ☐ Yes
    ☐ No

54. If no, why not? (tick all that apply)
    ☐ Family/friends would not approve
    ☐ Would not be treated well by the PSNI
    ☐ Would not be chosen due to my religion
    ☐ Would fear attack on myself
    ☐ Would fear attack on my family
    ☐ Would not be able to maintain contact with my family and friends
    ☐ Do not support the police
    ☐ Other (please state)..
    ....

Thank you for completing this questionnaire
ICR is an independent research organisation, which specialises in working on issues related to both conflict and post-conflict societies. The Institute is a recognised charity managed by a Board of Directors drawn from the community, voluntary and academic sectors. For more information contact ICR on 028 90 742682 www.conflictresearch.org.uk

Appendix 2
Police Ombudsman's procedure for complaining

Diagramatically

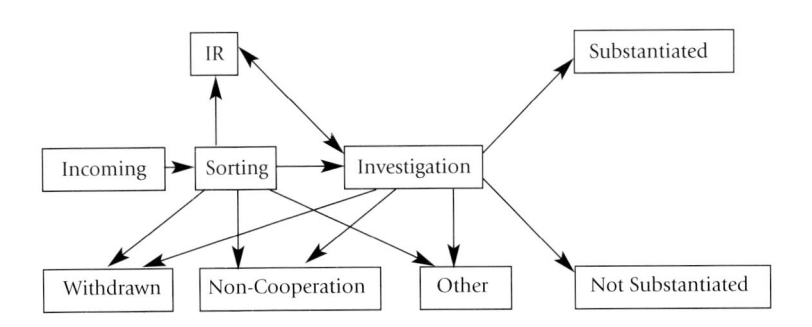

```
                IR ◄─────────────┐      Substantiated
                ▲                │      ▲
                │                │      │
  Incoming ──► Sorting ──► Investigation
     │          │   │       │  │   │
     ▼          ▼   ▼       ▼  ▼   ▼
  Withdrawn  Non-Cooperation  Other  Not Substantiated
```